RAISING
CHILDREN
to
Adore GOD

INSTILLING *a* LIFELONG
Passion for Worship

PATRICK
KAVANAUGH

 Chosen Books

A Division of Baker Book House Co
Grand Rapids, Michigan 49516

© 2003 by Patrick Kavanaugh

Published by Chosen Books
A division of Baker Book House Company
P.O. Box 6287, Grand Rapids, MI 49516-6287
www.bakerbooks.com

Printed in the United States of America

Library of Congress Cataloging-in-Publication Data
Kavanaugh, Patrick.
   Raising children to adore God : instilling lifelong passion for worship / Patrick Kavanaugh.
      p.   cm.
   ISBN 0-8007-9330-7 (pbk.)
   1. Worship (Religious education). I. Title.
   BV1522.K38 2003
   248.8′45—dc21   2003009314

Scripture is taken from the HOLY BIBLE, NEW INTERNATIONAL VERSION®. NIV®. Copyright © 1973, 1978, 1984 by International Bible Society. Used by permission of Zondervan. All rights reserved.

This book is gratefully dedicated to our dear friends,

Jim and Mary Jeane Kraft,

who have spent their lives
raising children to adore God.

Contents

Foreword

Beyond Education to Adoration

As parents we focus on every conceivable area of our children's lives in order to teach, guide and encourage them along the Way. We introduce them to the Bible with special cartoon versions of the New Testament, with videos and CDs. We try to acquaint them with missions by means of special Vacation Bible School youth programs. These are worthy areas of focus, deserving of our time and imaginative energy.

But how often are we handed back our children by these poor, overworked "ministry professionals" as unchanged and unmotivated as we ourselves continue to be? Have we not prayed enough? Have we missed out on a better program? Should the search committee have made another choice? Why are our children forever out of spiritual fuel? And why are we?

What we have failed to recognize is that in all areas of ministry, it is simple, pure adoration that fuels our hearts and souls for God. The Bible comes to life only when we read it as a love letter from the One we adore. Missions is a loving response of obedience by men and women who meet and fall in love with Jesus Christ and whose adoration overflows into the remotest corners of the world (and even next door!) The heart of worship is adoration. It is the beginning and end of our praise of God.

Now, back to our children, whom we left standing with their special kids' editions of the Bible, their CCM CDs, their invitations to the next "dynamic" youth conference. See the look askance in our direction? This look says to us, *TV and video games are much more interesting. Is there really more I should want?* They are longing for the key they don't even know how to ask us for. They are not merely children, after all; they are living souls—souls that, just like us, long to hear and discover the *what* and *why* of their own existence.

Are you prepared to show them? Am I? Can we open this door for our children when too many of us have rarely ventured to reach up and even touch the latch for ourselves?

The key— their purpose and ours—is to adore the living God, to embark on a lifelong journey of personal adoration.

So now you sit there (or stand there) with this book in your hands. You pulled it off the shelf because the title intrigued you and drew you in, perhaps hinting at the answer to a question you did not even know to ask. Our brother Patrick is handing us a long-term spiritual strategy, well thought out, non-programmatic and distinctly biblical. He invites and encourages us to adjust and adapt it for the differing needs of our unique children. More than the answers he provides in this book, he teaches us how to ask better questions—for our children's sakes and for our own.

So I encourage you to listen to him. I hope you will be convicted, as I was, to embrace the deeper calling we have as parents—not simply to other human beings, but to living, eternal souls; beyond education to adoration. Who knows but that, in the process, that door will at last swing fully open in our own lives as well, that we might join our children and together with them, on our knees, learn the lesson we have sought so long to teach them?

MICHAEL CARD

Introduction

*I*n the months following the release of my book *Worship—A Way of Life,* I was interviewed on dozens of Christian radio talk shows. From many different parts of the United States and representing a variety of denominational backgrounds, the talk show hosts asked a wide assortment of questions about worship, both public and private.

Yet there was one recurring theme that found its way into every program. Not a single interviewer failed to ask—on his or her own initiative—a question along the lines of "How can we *teach our children* to adore God?" A very significant question indeed!

THE NEED OF THE HOUR

Let me begin by saying that every believing parent should endeavor to pass the Christian faith along to each of his or her children. The result will be the children's eternal salvation, as well as a life of knowing and serving the Lord. As soon as one becomes a parent, this "passing of the baton" must become a supremely important aspect of his life.

This God-given responsibility is emphasized repeatedly throughout Scripture. From Moses' command about God's laws, "Impress them on your children" (Deuteronomy 6:7), to Paul's admonition to "bring [children] up in the training and instruction of the Lord" (Ephesians 6:4), the Bible is clear on this subject.

It is a sad commentary, then, that some Christian churches over the last few centuries have not encouraged this teaching. The British poet and philosopher Samuel Taylor Coleridge was once entertaining a man who insisted that any religious training of children was infringing on their liberty to express themselves and choose their own way. Coleridge refrained from arguing but led the man into his own rather neglected garden. His visitor was astonished.

"Do you call this a garden? There are nothing but weeds here!"

"Well, you see," the poet replied dryly, "I do not wish to infringe upon the liberty of the garden in any way. I was just giving the garden a chance to express itself and choose its own production."

In our own secular times, such "expansive" ideas continue. They may be considered politically correct, but they are biblically *in*correct.

Some years ago, I was talking with a new father who claimed, although he himself was a Christian, that he was going to allow his children freedom to "find the truth for themselves." He was not going to offer any parental guidance through their young lives. This well-meaning friend was rather shocked when I pointed out: "Unfortunately, the devil does not have such scruples." The world around us is all too happy to influence our children—and to do so powerfully—away from the faith.

Raising children to develop a sincere and personal faith in Jesus Christ is the need of the hour. If, from the dawn of Christianity, all believing parents could have somehow been successful in passing their faith to each of their children, most of the world would have been following the Lord for centuries. Perhaps the great evangelistic ministries and programs of our times would never have been needed. For as any evangelist gazes upon a crowd of potential converts, he is generally looking at individuals who have had Christians somewhere in their ancestry—but at some point the line was broken, the baton was dropped.

Before going any further, I want to emphasize two important points about instilling faith in children:

1. Some parents may do everything possible to encourage faith in their children, only to have this faith rejected. Children are ultimately free agents with free will and must answer individually to God Himself. This is a critical point for parents to remember, especially to avoid any false guilt. Even if we do everything right, some children will still deliberately rebel.

   For that matter, is this not also true of God's children? Our Lord is surely the *perfect* father, yet millions of His children have rejected Him. Concerning Jesus' coming into the world, the Gospel states: "He came to that which was his own, but his own did not receive him" (John 1:11). If people can rebel against the perfect parent, then our children can make the choice to rebel against us and our beliefs. Nevertheless, it is our job to do all we can to encourage their faith, trusting the Lord for the outcome.

2. Though we must raise our children in a way to inspire their faith, there comes a time when they must *make this faith their own*. As the old saying goes, "God has no grandchildren." For young adults to go to church simply "because their parents always did so" is not the right reason. This is fine for little children but not for men and women. Sooner or

later, each individual must make his own decision to follow Christ or to reject Him.

All too many young people sincerely believed the Gospel as children, yet did not successfully bring their faith into adulthood. Again, it is the parents' job to raise their children in such a manner as to encourage this crucial transition into dedicated Christian adults.

THE SUPREME PLACE OF INTIMACY AND ADORATION

"All right," you may concede. "I certainly want to see my children grow into adulthood as strong Christians. To this end I've been teaching them to pray and reading the Bible with them. But what do you mean about teaching my children *to worship?* Isn't that what we do Sunday morning at church?"

Now we come to the purpose of this book. As I wrote in *Worship—A Way of Life,* true worship is far more than what we do corporately at church. Indeed, in all too many churches, Sunday morning worship is virtually an *adult* experience, which leaves the children either confused or bored or both. As a minister of music, I have repeatedly looked out at congregations in worship and seen many parents heartily singing to the Lord—completely oblivious to their indifferent children, who clearly would rather be elsewhere.

No, this book is not about that kind of "worship."

Every one of us was made to worship God every day in our homes, offices, cars—wherever we find ourselves. And the purest form of worship is *private adoration.* This can take place anywhere, any time—it does not require a church, a choir, a song or even a Bible. It only requires a heart that wants to say directly to God: "I love You, Lord. I praise You for who You are. I thank You that You love me and call me Your child."

This is the attitude of heart that we want our children to experience.

Adoration is an intimate form of worship. It is not about singing, going to church or performing any outward rituals. It is about forming and nurturing an internal relationship with God.

For over two decades I have worked closely with Christian kids, as a principal of a Christian elementary school, a teacher in a Christian high school and now as director of the MasterWorks Festival (a summer arts camp of high school and college-age students). I have had the joy of seeing many young Christians bring their faith into adulthood, and I have known the anguish of seeing many others abandon their faith as they left childhood behind. Furthermore, my wife and I have raised four wonderful sons, all of whom deeply love Jesus Christ, yet each in his own way.

Again and again I have seen how the platitudes often heard today in Christian circles about child rearing do not work. Why? Because they generally involve certain outward things done in certain ways. That is, if we simply have our children go to church, sing the songs, memorize a few verses and put their coins in the plate—well, then, we have done our parental duty, right?

All of these things are good, of course, but they are not an end in themselves. They are the means toward a higher end: that of knowing God intimately. These external duties must be taught to our little children, to be sure. But as our children mature, they will need something deeper than outward functions. They will need to adore the Lord themselves. Otherwise, they become those whom both Isaiah and Jesus spoke against: "These people honor me with their lips, but their hearts are far from me" (Matthew 15:8). It is *the hearts* of our children that must be turned toward the Lord.

Unless young Christians develop this internal relationship with Christ, they will tend to see activities like reading the Bible and going to church as the remnants of an unenlightened childhood. This has been recognized throughout the ages by those who love Christ. Thomas á Kempis wrote in his centuries-old classic, *The Imitation of Christ:* "If we let our progress in religious life depend on the observance of externals alone, our dedication will quickly come to an end." And if these activities in our children's lives—important as they may be—are merely external, then they can be easily discarded as a part of childhood (like Santa Claus and the Easter Bunny) when childhood is over.

Individual adoration, on the other hand, lasts because it is purely internal. When someone is sitting alone in God's presence, adoring Him, speaking words of praise and thanksgiving to Him—this is the fruit of a genuine relationship with the Lord. It is the difference between doing some*thing* and knowing some*one.*

Children understand this. They might read the Bible and pray in order to please their parents. (And this is not a bad thing at all!) But the only basis for adoring God is having a personal relationship with Him. It does not really involve the parent. It is purely between the child and God.

This is the natural progression of teaching our children. As C. S. Lewis reminds us: "We feed children in order that they may soon be able to feed themselves; we teach them in order that they may soon not need our teaching." While they are in our care, we teach them to adore God so that—long after we are gone—they might spend a lifetime (or rather, an eternity!) worshiping Him.

Any young Christians who have spent years adoring the Lord in such an individual manner are much less disposed to abandon the practice once they become adults. They know the difference between true worship experiences and doing something "just because Mom and Dad said to." Worship "happens" because God is really here, and they know Him. This is the ultimate fulfillment of the verse "Train a child in the way he should go, and when he is old he will not turn from it" (Proverbs 22:6).

If this type of internal spiritual relationship is what you desire for your children, then I invite you to read on.

1

What Is Worship?

Every day I will praise you and extol
your name for ever and ever.

PSALM 145:2

This book is about teaching children to adore God. It is not meant to manufacture young worship leaders or ministers of music, but to inspire our children (including teens) to have a deeper, more personal relationship with Jesus Christ. It is not meant simply to encourage worship in the present, but to enable each of our children to accept the truths of the Christian faith as his or her very own for life.

For all those who have children in their care—whether parents, grandparents or teachers—this is one of the most important duties you will ever perform.

THE IMPORTANCE OF WORSHIP IN THE FAMILY

How does God feel about this matter? Concerning Abraham, the great patriarch, the Lord explained: "I have chosen him, *so that* he will direct his children and his household after him to keep the way of the LORD by doing what is right and just" (Genesis 18: 19, emphasis added). God gave Moses this word for His people: "Impress [the commands] on your children. Talk about them when you sit at home and when you walk along the road, when you lie down and when you get up" (Deuteronomy 6:7).

Billy Graham, one of the greatest evangelists of our time, has talked about the supreme value of teaching the faith to children: "The only way to provide the right home for your children is to put the Lord above them, and fully instruct them in the ways of the Lord. You are responsible before God for the home you provide for them." It is impossible to exaggerate the importance of teaching children to worship God, and the optimum place to teach them is at home, in the family setting.

Yet many parents have tacitly left this duty to others. Some Christian parents have opted to let their churches teach their children to worship God. As we shall see in later chapters, the local church plays a wonderful part in your children's spiritual lives, but it was never meant to usurp the place of the family.

There is simply no better place to teach a child to adore God. It is at home, not at church or school, that we learn our most significant values. Author and teacher Charles Swindoll tells us: "Whatever else may be said about the home, it is the bottom line of life, the anvil upon which attitudes and convictions are hammered out. It is the place where life's bills come due, the single most influential force in our earthly existence. . . . It is here life makes up its mind."

TEACHING THAT WILL LAST

During the Last Supper, Jesus' final meeting with His disciples before His death, our Lord said, "You did not choose me, but I chose you and appointed you to go and bear fruit—fruit that will last" (John 15:16). The implication is that our fruitfulness is measured, not by its quantity but by its *permanence*. Often this principle is applied to evangelism. That is, if you lead someone to Christ, then you should continue to encourage him or her to follow the Lord throughout life. Jesus did not command us to collect "decision cards" but to make disciples.

In the same way, our responsibility as parents is to inspire a *lifetime* of worship. If our children politely go to church with us and sing all the songs and memorize all the appropriate verses but then abandon Christianity when they reach adulthood, our fruitfulness has been negated. Consider how the following parable relates to parenting. Jesus asked, "What do you think? There was a man who had two sons. He went to the first and said, 'Son, go and work today in the vineyard.' 'I will not,' he answered, but later he changed his mind and went. Then the father went to the other son and said the same thing. He answered, 'I will, sir,' but he did not go. Which of the two did what his father wanted?" (Matthew 21:28–31).

His listeners answered, "The first son," and Jesus affirmed their conclusion. God is not as interested in an initial avowal as He is in our long-term, lifetime response. Do you recall the parable of the sower? One of the areas of ground that was seeded contained more rocks than rich soil. The plants grew up quickly but soon wilted. Jesus compared this to someone who "hears the word and at once receives it with joy. But since he has no root, he lasts only a short time" (Matthew 13:20–21).

In raising children to adore God, we should always keep our eyes on the long-term goal. Will the seeds we plant take root? This is a mission that will not be accomplished in a day, a week or a month. It is a *lifestyle* of worship we are attempting to inspire. Teaching and modeling this subject effectively will take some adjustments in our own lifestyles.

As Christian parents, our hearts' desires are for our children to follow the Lord. We want this, not only because it is God's will, but because we know the joy of a relationship with the Lord. Yet it is one thing to know something for ourselves and quite another to be able to impart it to others. As Cicero once claimed: "Not only is there an art in knowing a thing, but also a certain art in teaching it."

In order to teach anything effectively to anyone, we need solid footing in two areas:

1. *The subject*—We must truly know the subject matter ourselves, what it is and what it is not.
2. *The teacher*—We must demonstrate the significance of the subject by believing in it, living it out in our own lives before the eyes of the students.

We will never teach our children to adore God without these two prerequisites. This opening chapter concerns the first point, making certain we all know what worship truly is and what it is not. The second chapter also focuses on us—the adult, not the child—to show how worship is taught by example and modeling, not by lectures! Let us begin, then, with the first prerequisite: worship.

WHAT EXACTLY IS WORSHIP?

The English word *worship* is derived from the Anglo-Saxon *weorthscipe*, which means "worthy," "worthwhile" or "having worth." This concept is simple: to be worshiped, one must have worth—one must be worthy of being worshiped. Christians attest to the fact that our great God is worthy of all adoration. As the Scriptures remind us: "You are worthy, our Lord and God, to receive glory and honor and power, for you created all things, and by your will they were created and have their being" (Revelation 4:11).

The best definition I have ever found for worship (*all* types of Christian worship) is this:

Worship is the individual adoration of God.

Thus, worship—adoration of God—can take place whether you are alone in a forest or singing along with your Sunday morning congregation. For even in the latter case, the worship is between each individual and the Lord. We tend to see the mass of people singing; God sees each individual heart: "Man looks at the outward appearance, but the LORD looks at the heart" (1 Samuel 16:7).

Indeed, if we are really honest about it, we can prove this by our own experiences. We all know that it is quite possible to be singing along in the congregation with gusto, yet our minds are a thousand miles away: at the office, in the home, at the ball game. Is this worship? Surely not. Worship is not merely a question of performing certain external actions; it is an *internal* service—the private adoration of God. Augustine reminds us: "When he is not worshiped alone, he is not worshiped."

As a minister of music, I have often looked at our congregation during times of worship. (All ministers of music do this; it's why we hit so many wrong notes!) Usually I see dozens of people singing the praises of God with all their hearts, showing every outward appearance of true worship. But sometimes I notice someone merely standing there, not singing, looking rather bored. It is all too tempting for me to assume that the person must not be in tune with God that morning.

Yet I cannot know this. Indeed, this person may be having a meaningful time of worship. Perhaps he or she is intensely aware of the presence of God and is standing in awe of the Creator. I have known many Christians who are devoted worshipers, yet are not the types to display the experience outwardly. In other words, you can be a worshiper without singing along with the congregation—you do not need a congregation. It is ultimately something that happens between you and God.

BUT WE WORSHIP GOD EVERY SUNDAY, RIGHT?

So, if true worship is an inward experience that can take place anywhere, you may ask, what is the problem? Just this. Most teaching about worship rightly divides the topic into two parts, corporate worship and individual worship. Both are found in Scripture and both are strongly encouraged. Yet today there is so much emphasis on corporate worship that many believers never consider worshiping God privately. In other words, they spend a half hour or so each week in corporate worship and trust that they are meeting God's call. They are actually limiting themselves to worshiping only when they have a church, congregation and musicians available to help them!

It is because of this practice, perhaps more than any other reason, that so many sincere Christian parents have such a difficult time teaching their children to adore God.

Think about it. If our children hear us *talk* about our wonderful, magnificent God but note that we worship Him only once a week, even the youngest children figure out that our actions belie our words. They conclude: "Why should I bother worshiping this God so much, when my parents seldom do so?" Whether we know it or not, we have just created a huge obstacle in the spiritual training of those in our care.

The private side of worship gives a very different message. It frees us to worship the Lord at all times, in all locations and in all circumstances. King David gives us the example when he proclaims: "I will extol the LORD at all times; his praise will always be on my lips" (Psalm 34:1). Note that he does not proclaim: "I will extol the Lord once each week; His praise will weekly be on my lips."

Before we begin training our children to worship, then, we must examine how *we,* as adults, worship. When I ask other Christians about their "worship life" they usually start talking about their churches and their Sunday morning experiences. Wonderful! But what about the rest of the week? Sometimes they mention daily quiet times. Wonderful! But what about the rest of the day?

God did not create us to worship once a week or even once a day. In the classic *The Practice of the Presence of God,* Brother Lawrence writes: "It is not needful always to be in church to be with God. We can make a chapel of our heart, to which we can from time to time withdraw to have gentle, humble, loving communion with him." He also taught: "We should fix ourselves firmly in the presence of God by conversing all the time with him."

We need to find ways of incorporating worship in all aspects of our lives: driving our cars, eating our meals, brushing our teeth, yes, even paying our bills. One of the most significant aspects of the Christian walk is to learn to worship the Lord more every day, to spend time with Him, to thank Him for all His goodness, to praise Him for who He is—whether you are in a church pew or a subway station.

This is true worship. This is what we need to be doing every day. And this is what we need to teach our children to do. Indeed, it would be rather odd to teach a child to worship God at church and nowhere else. To do so would be to teach him or her the lie that says that God is only at church and is not concerned with our lives from Monday to Saturday.

Please do not misunderstand me. This is not to belittle the importance of going to church! Each Christian should belong to a local fellowship, attending and supporting it faithfully. Furthermore, as we shall see in later chapters, worshiping at your local church is an essential part of raising Christian children. But our worship must extend far beyond the church doors. It must embrace our home, our work, our lifestyles.

Scripture admonishes us: "Through Jesus, therefore, let us *continually* offer to God a sacrifice of praise—the fruit of lips that confess his name" (Hebrews 13:15, emphasis added). How else will our lives convince our children of the supreme importance of worship? For our children *read us* every day. That is, they spend years casually observing their parents—what their parents do and how much time they spend doing it—forming a composite of their parents' priorities. We may have unwittingly taught them that Christianity is a Sunday affair, which really has little to do with "the real world."

The good news is that this can be changed! You can begin today on an adventure in worshiping that will lead you and your entire family closer to the Lord. You can decide this moment to make worship a higher priority in your life. Your children will soon notice the difference, and it will inspire them to follow in your footsteps.

Well, what should we *do* as we worship God every day?

Two areas are important for every believer.

1. Worship in Your Daily Quiet Time

Anyone writing a book faces the challenge of relating to the varied backgrounds of the readers. For example, many readers of this chapter may already enjoy private devotions or quiet times alone with the Lord each day. For many others, this may be a new concept.

To ensure that we are all thinking about the same subject, let me be specific. A "quiet time" is a regular part of the day in which an individual draws away from other duties and other people in order to spend time alone with God. Some of us have long quiet times; others of us have short ones. They can be at any time of the day or night, but they should be consistent. Again, David sets the example for us: "*In the morning,* O LORD, *you hear my voice; in the morning* I lay my requests before you and wait in expectation" (Psalm 5:3, emphasis added). Perhaps the most important thing is to rid yourself of distractions (this can be quite a challenge!) and focus entirely on the Lord.

What does one actually do in these quiet times? The answers may be as numerous as the number of believers alive today. Most Christians have two basic areas of concentration in their quiet times: prayer and Scripture. That is, each quiet time will consist of a combination of praying (supplication, thanksgiving, intercession, etc.) and reading (studying, memorizing, meditating on, etc.) the Bible. Keeping a spiritual journal is also beneficial.

Prayer and the study of Scripture are two of the most important areas of a Christian's life. Nevertheless, I would add a third area to one's daily quiet time: worship. That is, we should have a few moments when we set our Bibles aside, stop asking God for things and simply worship Him. One may speak praises to God, sing a song to Him or sit and quietly wait on Him. As we shall see in the next section, there are many wonderful ways to worship God—and we should incorporate them into our daily quiet times.

Those readers who already include quiet times in their daily schedules know the life-changing effect they have on the Christian walk. Those who have not yet tried this have a fantastic treat in store. I urge you to begin today! It will have a price, of course (like anything of great value), as you try to fit the time into your busy schedule. If it seems difficult to integrate this new aspect of the Christian life, remember the words of Scottish writer George MacDonald: "The doing of things from duty is but a stage on the road to the kingdom of truth and love." The long-term results of a daily quiet time will far outweigh the "cost."

Indeed, you will certainly want to incorporate this into your own life before trying to inspire your children to do the same—as we will see later in this book.

2. Worship as a Lifestyle

For many people, it may seem odd to speak of worshiping God while waiting in the supermarket line or while your computer warms up or while you sit in traffic. Perhaps they feel that these mundane activities are too unspiritual, too commonplace for worshiping the Almighty. Yet our lives were not made to turn off and on between the spiritual and the worldly. "The earth is the LORD's, and everything in it" (Psalm 24:1) and there is no time or place where our worship of God should be restricted.

Of course, this does not mean that we should routinely shout "Praise the Lord!" when we enter a restaurant. You may be carried out in a straitjacket! Many proverbs admonish us to be "prudent," and foolhardy brashness is not exactly a positive witness to the world. For that matter, God can hear what others cannot: "Sing and make music *in your heart* to the Lord" (Ephesians 5:19, emphasis added). Whether we make audible sounds or worship Him in our hearts, the Lord never misses a single word of praise.

How shall we worship God throughout our days? Here are a few ideas to help you begin (excerpted from *Worship—A Way of Life,* Chosen Books, 2001):

Speak praise to God (sometimes out loud, sometimes not)—In your own words tell the Lord you love Him, thank Him for His faithfulness, list His many attributes: "You are loving," "You are steadfast." Confess to God your gratefulness to be His child. Personalize verses that come to mind: "Let everything that is within me praise Your holy name!"

Sing songs to the Lord—Ask God to bring a song to mind that expresses your love for Him. It does not matter whether you are a good singer or not; what matters is that praise is unleashed from your heart. Concentrate on truly *meaning* the words you are singing, and stay focused on the Lord.

Sing spontaneous praise to God—Begin adding your own words of praise to songs, even if they simply repeat the same phrases. As you gain confidence, make up your own melodies as well as your own words. Do not worry about the musical quality of such improvising; concentrate on singing praise to God.

Do not neglect the physical—Lift up your hands to God. Kneel before Him. Bow down in reverence. Perhaps you will feel led to walk about, praising the Lord with every part of you. He created our bodies; He is not embarrassed by them as we sometimes are. Ask Him to lead you and encourage you in this biblical area of worship.

Give quiet adoration—There are also times to be quiet before the Lord in awe-inspired adoration. No words, music or motions are usually needed. These are times to, as David did, simply sit before the Lord (see 2 Samuel 7:18) and feel the joy of His closeness.

Meditate on the Word—The word *meditate* means "to ponder, to contemplate, to cogitate, to ruminate, to mull over, to reflect upon, to think about." Apply the above verbs to a line of Scripture and ask God to reveal Himself through this biblical concept.

Commune with God—Many of us think of the word *communion* as something formal or liturgical, but it simply means "to commune" with the Lord—that is, *to do normal things together with Him*. Eating—"breaking bread"—is an example. Many take "worship walks" with the Lord. Others do certain tasks—drawing, writing, sketching—as a worshipful time of communion with God. The important point is to be fully aware of the Lord's presence and guiding direction.

Wait on the Lord—A key part of worship is waiting on God. This is different from adoration in that waiting assumes a completely passive state. This is usually exercised after a time of prayer, of seeking the Lord's guidance. Once you have cleansed your heart by confessing sin and receiving His forgiveness, and have established a dedicated attitude of communion with God, stop and wait. Do nothing. But stay in a posture of worship and wait to see if God desires to direct you in any way.

None of these activities requires a church building, a choir, a sound system or a song leader. They require only a heart that wants to worship God whenever possible. Everyone's lifestyle is different, but we all have little moments during the day—in the shower, waiting for a red light, mowing the lawn—when we can say, "Praise You, Lord. Thank You for Your goodness to me. I love You, Father, and I worship You with all my heart."

To say such words only takes a few seconds. To incorporate such moments of worship into our days will utterly revolutionize our Christian walks. Always remember the truth spoken by the American president Calvin Coolidge: "It is only when men begin to worship that men begin to grow."

THE ESSENCE OF WORSHIP IS *RELATIONSHIP*

Why should we be worshiping whenever possible? Why should we be speaking praise or adoring the Lord during the workday? Does God really need all this worship?

Of course not. Scripture teaches us that an all-powerful God does not *need* anything. The reason that the Lord desires our worship is because *He desires a closer relationship with His children.* I do not sing songs of praise for musical reasons or meditate on God's Word for scholarly reasons. I am getting to know the author of the Book! Think about it. All relationships take time.

Consider your best friend. He or she was not your best friend the day you met. But over time you became close and your relationship was strengthened. The same is true concerning spouses. Many songs proclaim "love at first sight," but for most of us the courtship took a while. (For many of us, quite a while!) After the wedding, this special relationship will grow and deepen throughout their entire lives.

What about your children? If you desire to have a solid relationship with them, you will have to spend time with them. Not just "quality time" but quantity time as well! Indeed, as I look back over the years of parenting, some of our most memorable moments came unexpectedly—not because they were planned, but because we were together for a long time.

The building of all relationships takes time, and this is also true of the most important one: a relationship with the Savior. This is the essence of all worship. It is not to fulfill an obligation or execute a ritual, but to bring us closer every day to Christ.

This is exactly what we need to teach our children. And it is essentially teachable! The psalmist points out: "Blessed are those who *have learned* to acclaim you, who walk in the light of your presence, O LORD. They rejoice in your name all day long; they exult in your righteousness" (Psalm 89:15–16, emphasis added).

Parents should not be content simply to teach their children Christian songs in the midst of a congregation. We must inspire them *to worship God on their own each day*. That is our goal, and it can be done.

Now that we have defined the subject, let us consider exactly *how* it should be taught: the second chapter introduces us to the indispensable concept of modeling.

2

Modeling a Lifestyle
of Worship Before Our Children

Follow my example, as I follow
the example of Christ.

I Corinthians 11:1

*S*cripture is so utterly inspiring! It fills us with joy
and comfort, with gratitude and security. Our spirits
drink life from Scripture much as the roots of a tree
absorb water from the earth.

So do not get me wrong when I say that for many years
the verse given above irked me! The King James Version says
rather starkly, "Imitate me," and I usually cringed when I heard

it. "People are not supposed to imitate other people," I would protest. "I don't want people to imitate me; I want them to imitate Christ!"

Soon after the birth of our first son, I met with a wise Christian father in a weekly Bible study. When we came to this verse and I began my familiar refrain, he gave me some sobering news: "I'm afraid your son is going to imitate you whether you imitate Christ or not! You're *already* a model to him—you just have to decide whether you are going to be a good one or a bad one!"

Pow! The terrible truth of his words hit me like a ton of bricks. That was the day I first began to understand what parenting is really all about. It is not about how much money I make or how big my house is or whether or not I send my children to college. It is the daunting prospect of being an example that will be imitated—for good or ill. It is knowing that my actions from now on could make an *eternal* difference for my child. Gulp!

THE MODELING PRINCIPLE

"Don't do as I do! Do as I say!"

Have you ever felt like saying these two sentences to your children? I do not recommend it, of course. It would not work anyway. Our children will always learn more from the example of our actions than from all the pious preaching we can muster.

This leads to what I call "the Modeling Principle." It states:

We cannot expect our children to be any more dedicated to Christ than we are ourselves.

This concept is true of all "models" or "molds." When someone pours liquid metal or plastic into a mold, the form that emerges cannot be better (it may be worse) than the mold itself. When you place a piece of paper onto the glass of a photocopier, you do not expect the copy to be better (it may be worse) than the original. And a parent cannot with integrity expect, much less demand, that a child be a "better" Christian than he is himself.

Some will immediately object to this, arguing that children may indeed become more dedicated Christians than their parents. After all, they each have free will. And, obviously, many children of unbelievers become believers themselves. Is it not limiting the work of God to insist that no children can become more dedicated Christians than their parents?

Yes! Now look again at the Modeling Principle, for this is not what it says. Certainly, many children become more dedicated to Christ than their parents ever were. This principle asserts, however, that no parent *can expect* his or her children to be so. The Modeling Principle concerns the expectations we put upon our children, as well as the demands we make upon them.

EXPECTING MORE OF CHILDREN
THAN WE ARE WILLING TO DO?

Think about it. It is not right for parents to demand that their children pay a higher price then they are willing to pay themselves. Much of the Christian life involves making tough, sacrificial decisions—doing what is right, "even when it hurts" (Psalm 15:4). And much of the Christian life involves doing certain things consistently: praying, witnessing, reading the Bible, etc. We (correctly) tell our children to do these things. Are we doing them ourselves?

It is outrageous, for example, for a parent to insist that his children memorize Scriptures when the parent would never do so. Can we expect our children not to cheat on their school tests, if we cheat on paying our taxes? Should we tell our children to witness to their friends at school, if we are unwilling to witness to our colleagues at work?

No. This is the Christian version of the very hypocrisy that Jesus condemned in the Pharisees of His day: "Do not do what they do, for they do not practice what they preach" (Matthew 23:3). They should have been good models to follow, but they were not. In the same way, until we as parents model the basics of our faith, we can hardly expect to find these basics practiced by our children. English poet John Donne said it this way: "Of all commentaries of the scriptures, *good examples* are the best and the liveliest."

Obviously, an adult may do many things that a child may not. My twelve-year-old son may not drive my car, even though I do so. Differences might relate to health and well-being in various stages of life, such as a young child needing an earlier bedtime than a parent. Others have to do with maturity and experience, such as voting or joining the Army.

In this discussion, I am not talking about such obviously age-related actions. I am referring to the specific activities that are encouraged in Scripture for *every* Christian at *any* age. Different Bible teachers would probably disagree about the details of such a list. Let us assume that we agree upon these basics: prayer, the Bible, witnessing, holiness and worship.

For each of these (at the very least), the Modeling Principle holds. This puts the onus back where it belongs: on the parent. We need to examine ourselves (see 2 Corinthians 13:5) if we are to have a long-term impact on our children. Before attempting to change or influence our children in a specific area, we may first need to change ourselves.

Concerning worship, for instance, the Modeling Principle might read like this:

> We cannot expect our children to worship God consistently if we are not worshiping God consistently.

UNDERSTANDING DIFFERENT TYPES
OF AUTHORITY

This does *not* mean, of course, that children should be free to disobey whenever they see their parents model inadequately a behavior that is being demanded of the children! Whoa!

A Christian household cannot run properly without authority on the parents' side and obedience on the children's part. The Bible says: "Children, obey your parents in everything" (Colossians 3:20). When I tell my son to do something, I expect him to do it—*without* questioning whether I have been a good model for him or not! There are times to say to your children, "Because I'm the Dad (or Mom), that's why!"

This type of authority might be called *Authority of Position*. The reason that the child should obey this particular adult is that the adult has been placed in the position of parent. Whether he is a good parent or a poor one is not the question. Similarly, a private in the Army must obey his sergeant (whether a good one or not) because that person outranks him. In a manner of speaking, the private is not obeying the person himself but his position: He must obey *anyone* in that position.

Another type of authority might be called *Authority of Experience (or Knowledge)*. Consider the position of a wilderness guide in a familiar countryside. A stranger to that area might be a more accomplished woodsman, but if he does not know that specific terrain then he must submit to the authority of the guide or become lost. It is the authority of a knowledgeable teacher and carries with it great weight.

In the earliest days of child rearing, the parent obviously possesses this type of authority as well. The adult has had many more experiences and far more knowledge than a little child. As the child grows and becomes educated and experienced, the parent may lose some of this advantage (whether we want to admit it or not). It is an odd—and rather humbling—experience to be talking with your teenager about, say, world politics or computer technology, and suddenly realize that he or she knows more about the subject than you.

Now let us suppose that a parent and an older child are in an argument, and let us suppose further that it focuses on a topic of which the older child has more experience or knowledge than the parent. (It does happen, you know.) Some parents will resort to using the authority of position and insist upon submission. The Christian child is to obey respectfully, and parents who take this position will usually conclude that they have won the day—but at a high price that is all-too-often overlooked.

When someone is forced to submit in an area in which he or she is more knowledgeable, the overall effect is a lowering of respect toward the person of authority. A parent may coerce the short-term behavior from the more knowledgeable child, but in the long run this may result in a gradual erosion of the child's respect for the parent. An inexperienced sergeant may get the privates to obey him because of his position, but he will never inspire the invaluable qualities of loyalty and élan that an experienced sergeant can extract from his troops.

Now let us consider an even higher type of authority. As an example, consider the position of a successful football coach. He has been placed in authority and he doubtless possesses a great deal of knowledge and useful experience. But the coach has something far more valuable: He has a proven track record. He has a long line of successes, is recognized as an expert in his field and is, therefore, emulated by all who watch him. In short, he is *modeling* the art of coaching.

This type of authority might be called *Authority of Recognition*. It is so effective that players will try to get on this coach's team, even if they do not like him personally! This is why fine musicians want to play in an orchestra under a renowned conductor, though he may be a tyrant and an egotist. They recognize that his known genius will give everyone great musical results. This is the person of whom Seneca spoke when he said: "The greatest man is he who chooses right with the most invincible resolution."

Any true leader knows that this third type of authority is more valuable than the other two. When a person possesses authority of recognition, he or she embodies confidence and moral strength. People expect these individuals to do the right thing because they have a reputation for doing the right thing. Even if you disagree with this person, it is not difficult to submit since logic will tell you, "It's quite probable that he (or she) is right, and I am wrong about this."

This is the authority needed to parent properly and inspire our children to follow us in serving the Lord. As we seek to live the Christian life, God will bestow this authority upon us. As Scripture says, "There is no authority except that which God has established" (Romans 13:1). Over the years of parenting, if we have carefully attempted to model the Christian walk (showing humility, asking our children for forgiveness when needed, etc.) then we will tend to have more than simple obedience—we will win their respect. As we will see below, winning older children's respect becomes supremely important if they are to embrace a parent's faith as they enter adulthood themselves.

Winning an Argument Versus Winning Your Kids' Respect

Of course, winning respect will not eliminate all arguments between parents and children, for children of every age still want their own way. But winning their long-term respect is far more important than winning a short-term argument. This is especially true if the way you generally win arguments is by demanding submission because you are in a position of authority.

Granted, as I mentioned above, it is true that we may some-times have to rely on this position of authority and have the final say in the matter. It is hoped, of course, that when we resort to this technique we are sincerely looking out for the child's best interests and not just trying to meet our own ego needs—to appear as the big, important adult whom children obey. Parents who rely too much on their authority of position often find that when their children are older they finally throw off this yoke, rejecting both the parents and their belief-systems. This is undoubtedly a major reason why so many kids from Christian homes do not carry their faith into adulthood.

Yes, it may be easier in the short run always to demand teen-agers' submission, and sometimes you simply have to. But it is better to cultivate their respect by modeling the Christian life (more on this below). In this way, we tend to *inspire* obedience rather than simply demand it.

Why is this so important? Because earning long-term respect from your children—especially teenage children—will enable them *to respect your belief system as well*. This may be the most critical factor in whether or not your Christian child will someday become a Christian adult. It is the most important step toward teaching your children to worship God.

What, Then, Are We to Model to Our Children?

To answer the above question, we need to consider two basic categories. The first is concerned with actions and attitudes that could be labeled "virtuous." They include loving your spouse, showing compassion, humility and patience, curbing anger, encouraging those around you, avoiding hurtful speech, using self-control.

This list could go on and on, but you get the idea. All of these actions and attitudes are found throughout Scripture and form a central part of living the Christian life. Indeed, to display such virtues consistently can only be done by the power of Christ working within us.

You will notice that this list encompasses many concepts that have been embraced by non-Christians. There are many atheists, for instance, who believe in showing compassion, humility and patience. These traits are, of course, founded upon God's Word, but they are also found in the teachings of many other societies. In other words, this first category of virtues that we are to model contains many actions and attitudes that are not *specifically* Christian—even though every Christian should put them into practice.

Contrast this with the second category. This includes such actions as reading and studying the Bible, praying to God, worshiping Jesus Christ. Behaviors like these are foundational for every Christian; indeed, we would not do them if we were not Christians. Muslims do not study the gospels. Hindus do not pray to God for help and guidance. Atheists do not worship Jesus Christ. Further, actions in this category are uniquely motivated by Christian love: "And over all these virtues put on love, which binds them all together in perfect unity" (Colossians 3:14).

So we as parents must model the Christian life for our children by modeling *both* of the above categories—the "virtuous" and the Christian. We will not be successful in passing on our faith if we only use one category and not both. For example, if you model reading the Bible but never exhibit compassion and humility, you will actually teach your children hypocrisy, since you are reading the Bible but not doing what it says. Likewise, if you model compassion and humility but never emphasize the importance of God's Word, you may raise a kind humanist, but not a biblical Christian.

Children need to get the whole package. An art student does not focus forever on only the color green; he must learn to work with the entire spectrum of colors. In the same way, if we are to teach our children to worship and adore God, we must teach them how true worship is a vital part of the balanced Christian life—and we do it best by example, by consistently modeling the balanced Christian life for them to observe.

HOW DO YOU TEACH SOMETHING THAT IS INTERNAL?

We now see the truth of the Modeling Principle: There is no use telling your children to worship God if you are not worshiping God. Furthermore, children need *to know* that you are worshiping. But how can this happen, since, as we saw in the first chapter, worship is essentially internal? They cannot *see it* when you are worshiping in your heart.

The first answer to this problem has to do with the way we talk about worship. Since our children need to be shown that worshiping is a natural part of the balanced Christian life, it should be referred to often in daily conversation—but not as something unusual. At the dinner table a parent might comment something like, "I was taking a moment to worship the Lord today at lunch, when the most interesting Scripture came to mind."

Note that the parent did not say, "I want to talk to you children about the importance of worshiping God." Worship was referred to in passing as a natural event. To say much more would make it seem like an unusual occurrence or, worse, sound like a lecture. Remember the words of French writer Jean de la Bruyere: "The great charm of conversation consists less in the display of one's own wit and intelligence than in the power to draw forth the resources of others."

Another answer to the question of how to teach something that is internal has to do with its external manifestations. One generally learns by the assistance of outward aids and over time the aid ceases to be needed as the practice is internalized. Young music students often learn their music with a metronome ticking in the background, but it would never be present in a performance. Once the rhythm is internalized, the metronome is unneeded. In the same way, a parent will often teach worship by initially focusing on outward actions, such as singing or kneeling. Later, as the child becomes more familiar with the Lord they are worshiping, the teaching emphasis shifts to the internal. We will spend much more time on this in later chapters.

Let me mention here, though, one particularly important outward action: speaking praise. Children are deeply influenced by our words. It should be a normal and natural thing for them to hear us say such biblical expressions as "Praise the Lord!" or "Glory to God!" We do not have to be overbearing about this, but the Bible does say: "My mouth is filled with your praise, declaring your splendor all day long" (Psalm 71:8).

If a practice like speaking praise is new to you, I do not recommend that you immediately begin yelling "Praise God!" throughout your house. Your children will assume that you have lost your marbles. Teaching and learning are gradual, long-term processes. As you pick up ideas in this book and others that strike you as worthy for your situation, I advise you to work them into your daily life *gradually*.

YOU MUST STILL BE LEARNING, TOO

The example above about speaking praise brings me to yet another point about modeling the Christian life. We all want our children to learn; in fact, we want them to *want* to learn. What better way than for us to *model* learning! Acting as if we know it all is always a turnoff; our children are not stupid—they know better. Instead, we should live out the truth of Proverbs 9:9: "Instruct a wise man and he will be wiser still; teach a righteous man and he will add to his learning."

If our children see that we are actively involved in the joy of lifetime learning, then they will catch the same magnificent passion. One of my favorite quotes is by the writer Harvey Ullman: "Anyone who stops learning is old, whether it happens at twenty or eighty. Anyone who keeps on learning not only remains young but also becomes constantly more valuable." This principle can affect many diverse aspects of child rearing, and it particularly aids us in our endeavor to teach our Christian faith.

My wife and I seldom sit down at the table with our children without bringing up something we learned that day: from a book, a tape, a conversation with a friend, a story we heard on the radio. We want to establish before our children the fact that we are still learning, and that we love the quest of learning. Sometimes these comments concern natural phenomena, but they are about spiritual aspects of our lives, too. We might, for instance, share some new facet of a certain verse that we discovered in our quiet times or heard in a sermon.

The way you respond to what your child is learning is equally important, particularly when it has to do with the Bible. Always remember: If your child offers some tidbit he has perceived, never belittle it with your superior knowledge or experience. Instead, say, "That's marvelous! What a fascinating thought!" You will have just planted a desire to search out the truths of God's Word and then share them with others.

In fact, even if your child brings up something that is doctrinally ridiculous, try not to look shocked or to quickly shut it down. (To do so will often give the child something erroneous to defend as his own!) It is better to give a thoughtful reply such as, "That's interesting. But I wonder how this idea could harmonize with the biblical teaching of. . . ." Then gently bring the conversation into the ways of the Lord.

Ultimately, we believers are *all* students, learning as best we can on the same road toward the Lord. We parents may have had a few more years at it than our young children, but we have much to learn. We need to know more of God every day and to convey that spirit of learning to our children. When they see that we want to learn how to worship the Lord with greater fervor and enthusiasm, they will want to learn as well.

MODELING THE CHARACTERISTICS OF GOD

Let us now consider a most important aspect of modeling: modeling the various characteristics of the Lord. Here are two examples to show you what I mean.

Justice is one characteristic of God's nature that can be modeled. It is not only what He does, it is part of who He is. Therefore, parents must create a home life in which justice reigns, where the children know that doing good will be rewarded and that doing wrong will be punished. Parents must demonstrate the quality of justice, not simply to keep peace in the house (though that sounds great, too!), but to exhibit the justice of the Lord.

Unconditional love is another characteristic of God that can be modeled. Scripture teaches that "God demonstrates his own love for us in this: While we were still sinners, Christ died for us" (Romans 5:8). If parents show only conditional love—that is, love given only under certain circumstances—the children's view of God's love will be distorted. They may grow up believing that they must "perform" to deserve love from the Lord.

In many ways, modeling God's nature is ultimately what parenting is all about. Parents do not make children pick up their toys solely to have a clean house but also to teach that

41

"God is not a God of disorder but of peace" (I Corinthians 14: 33). Individuals will likely disagree about what specific aspects of godliness should be emphasized above others; I will leave such details to you. Meditate on those facets of the Lord that mean the most to you and the way you believe God wants you to raise your children.

You see, these principles must be adapted to every family and every child throughout every age of childhood. Many aspects of parenting are spelled out in Scripture, but others need to be considered prayerfully; forcing someone to obey a man-made rule as if it were Scripture is a dangerous business. Thus, if specific guidelines for a particular situation are not given in Scripture, we must examine the general principles that are given and ask the Lord to lead us as we apply them to our own circumstances.

All child rearing is a challenge, whether you have one child or twenty. Sometimes siblings seem determined to terminate one another. After having several boys, my wife and I learned that silence (at least, from their rooms) was not always golden—and could mean trouble brewing. We jokingly used to change the last word of Proverbs 29:15 to make it more descriptive of our household: "A child left to himself brings grief to his *brother!*"

Now that we have covered the introductory information— about worship itself and how we as parents must model whatever we teach—let us delve into the many practical aspects of teaching children to worship the Lord.

3

Knowing Your Children

*Be sure you know the condition
of your flocks, give careful attention
to your herds.*

PROVERBS 27:23

As we enter the next section of this book and shift our focus to our children specifically, let us remember that the goal is not for them to sing Christian songs for a few years in their youth—only to go their own ways as they grow up. No, the goal is to see our children grow into men and women who adore God as adults. To strive for this higher goal means to embrace a long-term parenting strategy and to be deeply involved in our children's lives every step of the way.

Very few of us live on the farm these days, so the above verse may not seem to have much relevance. Yet for all of us who have children in our care, the principle behind this verse is of supreme importance. You may not possess flocks or herds like Israelite nomads, but if you have children, you had better know about their condition.

Of course, for those of us who have large families or teach in classrooms, the word *herd* may still have significance!

Heredity Versus Environment

If you tell parents that they need to know their children, you will, of course, receive nods of agreement. Yet few truly realize the vast importance of this complex subject. Botanist Luther Burbank, observing the typical parenting in his community, once remarked: "If we paid no more attention to our plants than we have to our children, we would now be living in a jungle of weeds."

It is a subject requiring great attention because, as parents of multiple children soon find out, *every* child is unique. It never ceases to amaze us how the children of the same two parents can turn out so differently! This can be true in virtually every aspect of their lives.

Many factors contribute to this phenomenon, but the most significant have to do with (1) heredity and (2) the environment. The first is a complex issue, since a child's genes result from a wide-ranging pool. A child is not simply the "product" of two parents; he or she carries the traits of countless grandparents, great-grandparents and so on. Often I look at my own children and detect characteristics—not of their mother or father—but of an uncle or distant cousin.

As to the second factor, children's environment plays a huge role in shaping character. What I call *environment* includes everything in your child's life, from his birth order to his siblings to his household to his church, school and friends. All these diverse factors can produce amazing variations in your children.

At times, for instance, it seemed that if you asked our second-born son about his favorite things, he might have responded genuinely: "Whatever my older brother *doesn't* like." They were not antagonistic toward each other; they were quite good friends. But the second born felt the inner need to find an identity that was distinct from his older sibling's.

In the same way, two siblings will often react in opposite ways to the same environment. I once heard the story of two daughters of an alcoholic father. One girl became an alcoholic while the other remained a fastidious teetotaler. When asked separately why they took their paths, they gave *the same answer*—though they meant it in two very different ways: "What do you expect, having been raised by an alcoholic?" One daughter sadly took for granted her father's example, while the other looked at the pain it caused and abhorred anything to do with intoxicants.

Of these two fundamental components, there is nothing you can do about one of them—heredity; the genes are already in there! But there is much you can (and should) do to affect the environment. Indeed, this is a monumental responsibility for every parent. This chapter and the next will examine the "inner" and "outer" sides of your children's environment.

Your Flocks and Herds

What does it really mean to "know the condition of your children"? Most parents fall somewhere between remembering their names and being privy to their innermost thoughts. Obviously, some of us are better at this than others.

Consider this humorous quiz for fathers I once heard. The scene is as follows: Dad wakes up one morning next to his very pregnant wife. She tells him she is sick and asks him to get the children something to eat and send them off to school. Which of these three answers comes from the sleepy dad's mouth?

1. "Um, you mean, like find them some cereal or something?"
2. "Um, you mean they're already going to school?"
3. "Um, you mean there's three of them?"

We may laugh at this, but the question remains: How well do we really know our children, each one of them? The importance of knowing all we can about "how our children tick" (*why* they act and speak as they do) becomes even more essential as we seek to encourage their relationship to God through worship.

What Is Your Child's Ideal Instrument?

Here is an interesting way to illustrate this principle. As a musician who has worked with thousands of children, I often get the following question from young parents: "Which musical instrument should my child start with?"

This is truly a complex question. There are practical factors, such as the distance between your home and a good teacher of such and such an instrument. If your next-door neighbor plays clarinet in the local orchestra, perhaps your child should take clarinet lessons. There are physical factors. If your child is wearing braces, better not count on a French horn; how about a violin? You may lean toward the harp or organ, but do you have access to one or can you afford to buy one? There are many other factors to consider that really have no relevance for this book.

Yet there is a major factor that has everything to do with it: your child's *temperament*.

While talking with young parents about this subject, I always inquire, "What type of temperament does your child have?" If I get blank looks, I suggest, "Tell me about your child's personality." Sometimes further prodding is needed: "Is your child quiet or boisterous or exacting or laid back or what?"

You see, the answers to these questions can have a powerful effect on the success or failure of a young musician. If your daughter is reserved or inhibited, it would be a disaster to make her play first trumpet—where every little mistake is heard by all. Perhaps she would find strength and confidence playing in the string section of the orchestra, playing the viola or cello. In other words, you should take your child's temperament into account when choosing the right instrument.

Do you truly know your children's temperaments? Temperament might be defined as the "inner side" of an outward personality. This is often difficult to discern in children—or in adults, for that matter. This is not a new problem. Proverbs 20: 5 points out that "the purposes of a man's heart are deep waters, but a man of understanding draws them out."

Often parents will know what their children like and dislike, but they have no idea *why*. That is, why do the children like or dislike certain things? What are their feelings behind such preferences and the actions these preferences dictate? These thoughts and feelings within your children might be called the inner side of their environments.

Skillfully asking this wonderful word *why* can be a very effective way of knowing your children better. Don't simply ask: "What is your favorite color?" Follow it with a friendly: "Why is that?" Prod children into explaining (perhaps to themselves for the first time as well) the reasons why such and such is a favorite color. And, of course, whatever they say—no matter how illogical it may sound to you—never belittle the answer. You want to show that you always have a genuine interest in knowing them better.

47

In All Things, Respect

This leads to perhaps the most important aspect of environment, particularly in homes with multiple children: respect—that is, respect for all. This even includes things we do not like about our children. Gulp! Most young parents naively assume that they will always like the stages their children will pass through or even remain in. We have no such promises before us. Frankly, it is easy to respect those with whom we are in complete agreement, but what about those we do not admire? Can we still show respect and acceptance?

Let me give a real example to illustrate this idea. I know a Christian family that is presently in considerable turmoil. Their first three kids were model children, achieving everything their Type-A parents desired and following in the footsteps of the parents' likes and dislikes. The parents were visibly proud of these children. Then Billy came along. He has never been the least bit rebellious, but he seems different from the other children. He likes to wear "hippie-style" clothes and has a laid-back personality. He truly loves the Lord, reads his Bible daily and has a strong prayer life. But he does not fit in very well with tie-and-coat suburban Christianity.

Billy's parents are pulling their hair out. They are ashamed to sit with him in church. They have tried everything to make him change. What they do not realize is that *they* need to change. They need to show Billy that they love and respect him just as he is. They have confused the genuine reality of Christianity for its outward appearance at a given time in a given part of the world.

Please note that by *respect* I do not mean letting children do whatever they want! As I mentioned earlier, the Bible insists that children obey their parents in everything, for this pleases the Lord (see Colossians 3:20). Parents are to set rules (which must be *based upon scriptural principles,* for that is where their authority comes from!) and see to it that they are obeyed. This can never be compromised without negative consequences.

In other words, if their children are doing things that are forbidden *by God's Word*—lying, stealing, fornicating, showing disrespect, etc.—then parents must put a stop to it immediately. Renowned preacher Charles Haddon Spurgeon used to remind his congregation poetically: "When home is ruled according to God's word, angels might be asked to stay with us, and they would not find themselves out of their element."

Children will probably display personality traits or have tastes that are different from their parents'. Know that this is not the same as breaking God's law. Indeed, it is a time for deference and respect. The Lord's Kingdom is large enough for all types of people *who obey the dictates of Scripture*—whether they are straight-laced banker types or laid-back hippies, whether they listen to Bing Crosby or the Newsboys. And if the children see that their parents respect each one of them, they, too, will learn to respect each other, and later transfer this respect to others.

One reason parents need to show equal respect for every child (including those who do not have the same likes and dislikes) is to avoid the formidable snare of favoritism. Remember the story of Jacob and Esau? How Mom (Rebekah) loved Jacob but Dad (Isaac) loved Esau? (See Genesis 25:28.) All that the parents succeeded in doing was to make enemies out of their two sons. What a different story it might have been if each parent had loved and respected both sons equally!

KNOWING HOW YOUR CHILDREN FEEL INSIDE

Thus we begin to understand why this concept of "knowing our children" is so important. Anyone who has been involved in counseling finds that most of us (yes, this includes Christians) tend to hide our inner struggles from even our closest friends.

We go to church and greet fellow believers with a smile, giving the outward impression that things could not be better. Yet we may be agonizing inside, or feeling worthless or depressed, or hating God—being careful to give no clue of this anguish to our colleagues.

In the same way, our own children may be going through terrible periods of pain or depression, and, because they often hide their troubles, we might be oblivious to it. Think about it. When they see everyone else walking around with a smile, they really assume that everyone else is happy and that they are the only ones with all these problems and doubts.

Who will help them with these painful issues? Who will break through the veneer of a smiling face to bring comfort to a hurting youth? Obviously, it is principally the responsibility of parents to play this very Christlike role for each of our children.

We cannot leave this obligation to our children's teachers, counselors or friends. We play the role of the "Good Shepherd" of the sheep, as seen in Jesus' teaching of John 10:1–16. All others—though they may be important—ultimately play the role of the "hired hands." When the wolf comes (that is, trouble or pain), it is the good shepherd and not the hired hand who comes to the rescue of the sheep.

When I look around a busy street or a crowded office or a church lobby, I see many faces. Because of what I know about people from experience with counseling, I can assume that many are hurting inside. Yet I cannot possibly help them all.

On the other hand, if I sense that one of my children is hurting and I do not bring him comfort and good counsel, I have failed in one of the most significant responsibilities of parenting. I may be providing for my family a home, clothes, food and education, but those are physical things that could be given to them by others. Our higher calling as parents is *to know how our children feel* and to be ready to bring them the love and encouragement they need.

Many of us will struggle with this part of parenting. The reason is painfully simply: In order to truly know our children, they must truly know *us*. That is, we as parents must be open before our children. The Modeling Principle in the last chapter points out that we cannot expect our children to be any more vulnerable and open to us than we are vulnerable and open to them. This does not mean that we have to expose every gory detail of our fallen nature! But it does mean that we walk in honesty and humility, being as approachable as possible, without a veneer of false superiority.

So when you ask your children how their days went at school, be prepared to share how *your* day went as well. This can be tough for us sometimes, but God will give grace as we try to do what is right. Remember that He is much more interested in seeing your children follow Christ than you are!

OUR CHILDREN'S PARENTS AND OUR CHILDREN'S GOD

Psychologists will forever debate the details of this topic, but there is basic agreement that the way children feel about their parents has a profound impact on the way they feel about God. This is perhaps the most overwhelming and terrifying part of raising children. I frankly wish it was not the case—it would get us off the hook as parents! But this fact of parenting cannot be ignored, especially if we want our children to adore the Lord all their lives.

Are there exceptions to this principle? Yes. Cannot God overrule in the hearts of children who have been raised by ungodly parents? Certainly. But are we, as Christian parents, to presume upon this? Can we sit back and say, "Well, if God wants our children to know Him, He will have to do it all Himself"? No, it is our responsibility to do the best job we can, attempting to demonstrate the love of Christ before those in our charge. We are the ones God has placed upon this earth to show our children what He is really like.

Does this mean that we parents have to "play God" for our children? Must we be omnipotent, omnipresent and never make a single mistake in the family? Thankfully, no! In fact, some of our best parenting occurs when we utterly blow it before our children and then have the humility to admit the mistake and ask for forgiveness.

We do not have to be perfect, but we should realize that *the attitude* our children construct toward us will usually transfer to their long-term attitude toward God. Shakespeare wrote truly: "The voice of parents is the voice of gods, and to their children they are heaven's lieutenants." Proverbs 17:6 states plainly that "parents are the pride of their children." This is the way it should be, as children's admiration for parents will be reflected in their worship of the Lord.

Some parents—particularly those who did not have a healthy relationship with their own parents—may find this reading uncomfortable, yet it is true. I have talked intimately with hundreds of Christians over the years and have seen it confirmed again and again. If a child feels far removed from the parent—whether ignored, unloved, misunderstood or unappreciated—then he or she will likely feel far removed from God. Consider the horrific ramifications of this: Who wants to worship a God who does not care? Maybe He is not there after all. Why bother about having a relationship with someone you are not even sure about?

Children whose parents were harsh or distant usually grow up to believe that God is harsh and distant. Children whose parents were overly permissive usually grow up to believe they can do whatever they want since the Lord will always forgive them anyway. And children whose parents were loving and just usually grow up knowing that we indeed serve a loving and just God.

What Do Your Children Think About God?

Now we see the supreme need to *know* our children, to be close to them, aware of what they are feeling. This type of parenting will demonstrate how close God is to us and give our children the knowledge that the Lord "will never leave you nor forsake you" (Deuteronomy 31:6). The child learns, through the parents' modeling, that he can always turn to God and that the Lord will always understand.

Every one of us needs this. It is an inner need that God places within us so that we might turn toward Him. It is why such Scriptures as Psalm 139 are so comforting: "O LORD, you have searched me and you know me. You know when I sit and when I rise; you perceive my thoughts from afar" (verses 1–2). It is also why Christ's terrible words to those who are not going to be saved bring such chills to us: "Then I will tell them plainly, 'I never *knew* you'" (Matthew 7:23, emphasis added).

Let us now bring this concept to a deeper level. Do you know how your children think about God? About heaven? Or hell? *Do* they ever think about such matters? Can you, indeed, *should* you encourage these thoughts?

To begin with, the answer to the last question is an emphatic yes! Colossians 3:1 commands us: "Set your hearts on things above, where Christ is seated at the throne of God. Set your minds on things above, not on earthly things." One of the great tragedies of our modern age is not that people are against God; rather they simply do not think about Him at all. Evangelists tell us that their greatest challenge is no longer opposition, but indifference to the Gospel message. The opposite of love is not only hate, but also indifference.

Yes, we should and we must encourage such thoughts in our children. How? To begin with, we should consider the preceding chapter: modeling. In other words, we must demonstrate frequently to our children that we are regularly entertaining thoughts of the Lord and not just thoughts of the office or the housework. Our children need to see that we are *thoughtful* and that our thoughts go beyond the laundry and the ball game. They must know from our lifestyles and conversations that we meditate on God's Word, that we ponder the mysteries He has created, and that we consider our roles of service within the world in which He has placed us.

FINDING A SPIRIT-LED BALANCE

There is a balance to find in all this, of course. One should not abandon all housework and sit poised like Rodin's statue "The Thinker." Soon you would not be able to *find* your children for all the clutter! Parents should, however, encourage the spiritual thoughts of their children by asking questions and having conversations that go deeper than usual small talk. This does not mean that all action stops and we sit and talk with long and serious faces. On the contrary, some of my best spiritual times with each child took place while we were throwing a ball, taking a walk or playing a game.

The key is to make such conversational transitions from the mundane to the spiritual as *natural* as possible. Children can easily detect when parents try too hard to sound spiritual, and they quickly put up a wall or fall asleep.

When our children were little, I sometimes noticed that whenever my wife began to bring something spiritual into her conversations with them, her voice would assume a higher "sing-song" quality. She reported that I often did the same. So when one of us fell prey to this oddly involuntary practice, the other parent would whisper our coded phrase, *vox humana* (Latin for "human voice"), a subtle hint to resume a natural-sounding conversation.

Incidentally we had many such code words in those days until our children became better at Latin than their parents! Oh, well, children are always motivated to outwit their parents!

WHAT ARE THEY *REALLY* FOLLOWING?

One final area concerning how well we know our children has to do with the final years of parenting. As your children grow up, the subject matter of your spiritual conversations must correspond to their ages. After seeing a movie with your four year old, you might talk about the importance of telling the truth or sharing with others. After seeing a movie with a fourteen year old, your topics may include standing up to peer pressure or keeping oneself pure.

Do not be surprised if, as your children mature, they develop different styles in their individual relationships to the Lord. I noticed this first in times of family prayer. One of the boys always prayed colloquially while another seemed to lean toward formality. Both were quite reverent and possessed a deep relationship with Jesus, but the difference in style was reflected in a number of subtle ways. It was a bit of "high church" and "low church" in the same house!

Is this so shocking? I said in the introduction that it is critical for all children to accept the truths of the Christian faith *on their own,* and not simply because their parents believe it. But this means that as they develop their personal faith, they may see things a bit differently. They may begin to interpret Scriptures in a manner different from ours. (Yipes!) Of course, this can (and should) result in a number of wonderful conversations, *if* we can resist the temptation constantly to shut them up with our "perfect theology."

This will be somewhat controversial, but it must be stated: We are striving to bring up *Christians,* not necessarily Christians within one specific denomination. We want them to have a personal relationship with Jesus Christ, not to a certain church slant. If they interpret certain Scriptures differently than you do, then praise God (and your children) for the time they are spending in God's Word!

Many of us are uncomfortable with denominations or churches other than our own. Generally, this is not because of doctrine but because of worship style. If we are Methodists or Baptists, it may dismay us to see our older children opt for Presbyterian or independent Bible churches (and vice versa). But to let such differences come between family members is a travesty.

Denominational differences give us a good opportunity to heed Romans 14:13, which commands: "Therefore let us stop passing judgment on one another." It is sad enough that the worldwide Body of Christ has divisions and arguments. Let us at least keep them from splitting our Christian families.

The best way to avoid this trap in the late years of parenting is to prepare your heart long before these years arrive. Determine beforehand to center your worship teaching on Jesus Christ, not on any particular slant on this subject. There are many wonderful Christian churches out there! As Oliver Wendell Holmes used to say, "All is holy where devotion knells."

Now that we have spent time examining the "inner" environment of our children, let us consider the many influences from their "outer" environment: their home, their church, their school and their friends.

4

Your Child's Environment
Home and Church

Train a child in the way he should go,

and when he is old he will not turn

from it.

*N*ow that we have examined the inner life of children, we need to consider their outward environment. Both are supremely important. Even if a child is in a "perfect" environment, parents need to know the child as well as possible. And even if parent and child are close, the child may still be strongly influenced by the environment.

Since our object is to inspire our children to worship the Lord—not only today, but as they become adults—our desire is to surround them with a healthy environment that will encourage this; those things that are around us continually have an immense effect upon our spiritual lives. Therefore, let us begin with the relationship between our outer environment and our inner lives.

WHAT GOES IN WILL COME OUT

Hollywood might try and tell us otherwise, but the principle works all the same: What goes in (our environment) will come out (in our words, thoughts and deeds).

In short, we are "influence-able" beings. This is why Scripture is specific about our influences, both positive and negative: "Do not conform any longer to the pattern of this world, but be transformed by the renewing of your mind" (Romans 12:2).

Much of the influence that gradually changes us is rather inconsequential and harmless. If you were raised in the South but move to the North, for instance, you will probably lose your Southern accent. If you are hired at an office in which everyone wears such-and-such style of clothing, you may soon do likewise. If you move in with a family that plays games each evening, you may begin to become a "game" person yourself, even if you have never enjoyed games before.

These changes do not happen because you are trying to make them happen but because of the ongoing examples all around you. Writer Edmund Burke once commented: "Example is the school of mankind, and they will learn at no other." Our surroundings influence us slowly but surely. These changes occur involuntarily, over time, often without our noticing. Indeed, the

Southerner who gradually loses his accent may not even know it until he returns to the South and is shocked to be called a Yankee!

Such environmental adaptations are innocuous, having little effect on our spiritual lives. Others, of course, can be much more harmful. Suppose a young Christian goes to college and finds himself surrounded by profanity. He never used foul language before but now feels out of place if he does not. He justifies it in his mind with an argument like, "Everyone else talks this way; I'll be ridiculed if I don't." Few young people are strong enough to hold out indefinitely against such an environment, and this student gradually adds swearing to his normal vocabulary. Just wait until he comes home to his Christian parents!

We are *all* affected by the things we take in, and the sooner we admit to this, the better. It amazes me to hear some people still argue that watching violent movies has "no effect" on us—even as violence in our society increases every year. When teenagers begin to hang out with druggies, they will usually descend in stages: (1) "They aren't such bad people"; (2) "Drugs aren't so bad"; (3) "Drugs can really be a good thing sometimes"; (4) "Pass the joint." There are exceptions, perhaps, but the principle of influence remains ever-present.

THE PRINCIPLE OF INFLUENCE

This principle might be stated like this:

In any given situation, you are either being influenced by others or you are influencing others or both.

As we grow older, of course, we tend to become more and more "set in our ways." That is, we become less influence-able each year of adulthood. But in youth this principle is seen in earnest. Children are still moldable, for good or for ill. It is during this critical period of influence—when our children are teachable—that we have our greatest opportunities as parents.

With this principle in mind, consider your own children at whatever age they are right now. Specifically consider those things that are within your control and those things that are out of your control. You can control, for example (at least, to some degree), your child's home environment, but you cannot control what his or her friends say or do outside of your home.

Our responsibility as "influencers" of our children, therefore, particularly if we want them to live a life of worshiping God, is twofold:

1. To give them the best Christ-centered environment within our control, modeling gratitude for and worship of God.
2. To teach them how to live a victorious Christian life—including worship—so that they will do so on their own when they are *out* of our control.

These two areas are all we can actually give our children (except for prayer—always an important part of parenting!). We cannot promise them a life without pain. Thomas á Kempis correctly noted that "there is no man in this world without some manner of tribulation or anguish, though he be king or pope." Therefore, it is a parent's responsibility to create a safe environment in which to grow up, and to teach children how to live rightly when they are out of that environment. But remember, we cannot control that outside environment and everything that it may throw at our children.

Therefore, how well we shape the environment that we can control becomes absolutely pivotal. In this chapter, we will examine the big picture of your child's primary environments: home and church. We will focus in later chapters on many additional aspects of the environment, but for now let us consider the ideals to which we are trying to aspire.

YOUR HOME—THE BIG PICTURE

What would you consider the ideal home life? None of us has it, of course, for the everyday realities of living tend to pulverize our households into the hectic lifestyles most of us lead. Nevertheless, we need occasionally to get back to basics and consider what we are trying to do in our homes. We may miss the target sometimes, but we at least ought to know where the target is!

This consideration of some of the attributes of a healthy Christian home may be painful for some, especially as we contrast these ideals to the less than ideal homes we may have been brought up in. Yet if we are to create a home atmosphere that will in turn encourage a lifestyle of worship, then we need to know the primary areas to emphasize.

In the previous chapter, we saw that a parent's modeling should revolve around the various aspects of God's character. Let us now take this principle into the development of a home environment. The particular areas to emphasize fall into five broad categories:

1. *Unconditional Love.* "But God demonstrates his own love for us in this: While we were still sinners, Christ died for us" (Romans 5:8). This includes forgiveness, acceptance, mercy, respect and encouragement; it is living in a "safe" place.

2. *Justice.* "He is the Rock, his works are perfect, and all his ways are just. A faithful God who does no wrong, upright and just is he" (Deuteronomy 32:4). No house, community, organization or country can survive without rules of

justice, where wrongs are punished fairly and doing right is rewarded.

3. *Wisdom.* "Oh, the depth of the riches of the wisdom and knowledge of God! How unsearchable his judgments, and his paths beyond tracing out!" (Romans 11:33). This category also concerns patience, humility, beauty, excellence and joy (that is, family fun!).

4. *Stability.* "I the LORD do not change" (Malachi 3:6). This speaks of the faithfulness needed in a parent, as well as spouses living in one accord, being consistent in discipline, working hard and sacrificing to provide for their family's needs.

5. *The Centrality of Jesus Christ.* "Jesus answered, 'I am the way and the truth and the life. No one comes to the Father except through me'" (John 14:6). This is not an aspect of God's character that we can model, but it is utterly essential to have a Christ-centered home if you desire to raise worshiping children.

1. Unconditional Love in Your Home

Once when one of our sons was home on a college break, he brought up a memory that made a strong impression on him. When he was a lad of four or five, our family happened to drive by a prison facility. I explained to him what a prison was and used the occasion for a short teaching: Don't be bad like those men! Yet my son remembers that I ended by saying, "But even if you went to jail someday, we would still love you."

All children need to *know* that their parents' love is utterly unconditional, that they do not have to perform for it and that it will never end. They need to know that even if everyone else turns against them, their parents will always be on their side. This supreme teaching should be spoken aloud (often) and demonstrated at every opportunity.

Some parents confuse this correct practice with the incorrect practice of permissiveness. If a child chooses to do something wrong, he should be disciplined appropriately. "Standing with them" does not mean bailing children out of punishments they deserve. Indeed, one of the ways we demonstrate our love is to take the time and effort for correction and show them the right thing to do.

God, the perfect Father, gives us the ultimate model. Describing how He will be a father to David, the Lord promises: "When he does wrong, I will punish him." Yet He adds, "My love will never be taken away from him" (2 Samuel 7:14–15). J. B. Phillips, the translator of the *Phillips New Testament,* described it this way: "God's love is not a conditional love; it is an open-hearted, generous self-giving which God offers to men."

Those who have been raised without knowing such love from parents often doubt throughout life that God truly loves them. But children who discover God's love and mercy early on have laid a cornerstone on which to build a lifetime of worship.

2. Impartial Justice in Your Home

When a child cries, "It's not fair!" he or she is expressing an inborn abhorrence of perceived injustice. Children demand justice for a very good reason: *No one* wants the terrifying prospect of living in a world without justice. We inherently want to know that if we are wronged, justice will be served.

This is why a child raised in a permissive home tends to grow up rather insecure. In the short run, she may delight in getting away with wrongdoing without penalty. In the long run, she lacks the conviction and security that result from a home in which correction is doled out consistently and fairly—and without delay.

If no one wants to live in a world without justice, then it follows that no one could really worship a God whom he thinks is unjust. Who could adore God with a grateful heart if he believed that God acts unjustly, whimsically or with partiality? One of the most profound statements in the Bible is found in three sublime words: "God is just" (2 Thessalonians 1:6). This is probably the ultimate prerequisite to being worthy of worship.

Yet this points out one of the toughest responsibilities of parenting. On one extreme, we have softhearted parents who cannot bring themselves (or take the time and effort) to discipline their children, even when it is clearly needed. On the other extreme, we have parents who punish in anger and are heinously abusive to their children.

There are many verses in the Bible that implore us not to "spare the rod" (see Proverbs 13:24; 22:15; 23:13–14; 29:15). Remember that these are not given simply to keep your children in line. They are to inspire us to model God's own justice, a part of His very nature. As our children are raised in virtuous and equitable homes, they learn to appreciate the Lord's embodiment of sovereign justice.

3. Wisdom in Your Home

Misconceptions surround the word *wisdom,* often confusing it with *knowledge.* Years ago the great English preacher Charles Spurgeon clarified this point: "Wisdom is the right use of knowledge. To know is not to be wise. Many men know a great deal and are the greater fools for it. There is no fool so great a fool than a knowing fool. But to know how to use knowledge is to have wisdom."

Nevertheless, for some of us the word *wisdom* still conjures up scenes of trekking up mountains in search of aged gurus. When such mental imagery confuses us, an ordinary dictionary comes in handy to clear the air. Wisdom is defined as "making good decisions based on experience and knowledge."

From a parenting point of view, this means that we must seek to make good decisions: the right thing to do, at the right time, in the right place. This is no small order!

As the Bible points out, "There is a time for everything, and a season for every activity under heaven" (Ecclesiastes 3:1). As parents, our duty is to discern *when* and *what* to do within our families. Should you let your teenage son grow his hair long? Should you let your daughter wear that short dress? Should your family spend the weekend with *that* family? Every parent will be confronted with thousands of such questions.

You will notice once again that the Bible does not specifically answer all of our questions. There are biblical *principles* to be examined, but exact answers are not always to be found. For instance, to the above question about the daughter's dress, the Bible speaks of modesty (see 1 Timothy 2:9), but it does not dictate how many inches above the knee constitutes modesty! It is up to parents to pray for God's wisdom in such situations and to make the best decisions they can.

The good news is that the Lord has given us an amazing promise in James 1:5: "If any of you lacks wisdom, he should ask God, who gives generously to all without finding fault, and it will be given to him." It is a shame that many rely on this promise only for a major decision or crisis. God's wisdom is available every day, for every parent, for every possible situation: Where shall we go on vacation? When should we start potty training? What time should be established as bedtime? etc., etc.

Of course, your children may not always appreciate your decisions. Dream on! But if they know that their parents consistently seek the Lord and have their best interests in mind, children will generally submit to decisions. They may disagree, of course, but they know from long experience that their parents are at least trying to do what is right for them.

Again, we see the importance of modeling the wisdom of the Lord, if we are to inspire worship in our children's lives. Parents' decisions guide the life of a child. God's guidance is available to the Christian who seeks to be in His will: "A man's steps are directed by the LORD" (Proverbs 20:24). How gratifying it is to worship a God who we know is looking out for our best interests!

4. Stability in Your Home

A common problem for young people today is the insecurity that comes from an unstable home life. Some of the worst scenarios include divorce, parental abuse and parental addiction. Such situations obviously can leave indelible scars on a child. Nevertheless, even children with two dedicated Christian parents can suffer similar pain unless the parents cultivate a safe and stable home.

It is sad to think how many ways parents place false guilt on the tender shoulders of a child. Statements like, "We would have so much more time if not for you kids!" or "All our money goes for our children!" or "Our last child was an accident." Words like these can be quite destructive. The message children receive is that they are unwanted. Because they realize that they had no control over coming into this world, they may soon begin to wish that they had never been born.

I have met newlyweds who do not want children because they have always heard—perhaps from their own parents— that kids are so expensive and so hard to raise. This common mindset should be shocking to anyone in the Body of Christ. After all, we are only in that Body because we were graciously adopted (see Ephesians 1:5) and at an expensive price: Christ on the cross.

The message a parent needs to send is this: "We are so glad that you are here!" and "Our lives are so much happier because of you." When a child feels appreciated, loved, accepted and safe within the family, it is much easier for him to develop a strong sense of gratitude—a key ingredient for all worship. When children are happy to be here, they become grateful to their parents for the stability they have created. This same gratitude will then be reflected on the Lord, and the thanksgiving they feel can lay the groundwork for a lifetime of worship.

5. The Centrality of Jesus Christ in Your Home

A particular bumper sticker used to be quite popular among Christians. It said: "If you were on trial for being a Christian, would there be enough evidence to convict you?" Consider for a moment. What exactly makes a Christian home *Christian?* As we saw in the second chapter, many worthwhile (and biblical) characteristics—such as honesty, generosity, humility and diligence—are evident in the homes of many non-Christians.

Ultimately, the one thing that makes a Christian home Christian is *the centrality of Jesus Christ.* It is not enough to teach your children to worship God just for the sake of worship. They must see Jesus as the center of their lives and worship their risen Savior. They must see Him as their salvation, pray in His name and tell others about Him. These are a few of the "crimes" that could convict someone of being a Christian.

All too often Christian parents attempt to teach their children about faith but wind up teaching religion. That is, we teach them that God wants us to be good, to pray, to go to church, etc. Perhaps these "crimes" could convict us as being religious—but not specifically Christian.

This is why the faith of some young people seems to fade out after they leave home. Their focus was not on personally knowing Jesus Christ; rather they acknowledged a vague God out there somewhere. The world will tell us that "everyone worships the same God" and that Jesus' exclusive claims are far too narrow. This lie will always cool the zeal of those who listen to it.

Indeed, who can worship such a God of vagueness? The essence of Christianity is that God "became flesh and made his dwelling among us" (John 1:14). Paul explains further that

Jesus is "the image of the invisible God" (Colossians 1:15). One of the many reasons for the incarnation is that we might give specificity to our worship, focus on the God-man, Jesus Christ. Martin Luther cut to the essence of this subject: "Anything that one imagines of God apart from Christ is only useless thinking and vain idolatry."

How do parents make their homes more Christ-centered? The answer lies in two directions. First, we should look inside and examine our own lives to see how *they* might be made more Christ-centered. Ask yourself: "What do I do regularly that only a Christian would do?" Whatever you give as an answer should now be done with greater frequency and fervency.

The second answer has to do with the outward expressions of parents' faith, and the home life we create. Ask yourself: "What is a regular part of our home life that would only be in the home of a Christian?" I look up from this computer and see a cross and a painting of Christ. I see Bibles and Christian books on the bookshelves. I think of the family devotionals we have after dinner and the conversations we have about the Lord.

Like thousands of other parents, I need to re-ask the first question constantly: "How can I make *my life* more Christ-centered?" All those crosses and Christian books in our house will make little difference unless our children see Jesus in the life of their parents. In the final analysis, the Christ-centeredness of a home will always be a reflection of the leadership of that home.

YOUR CHURCH—THE BIG PICTURE

Now that we have examined the home as your child's principal environment, let us consider another level of his or her world: your church. Like your home, your church is a place shared by both parents and children. Unlike your home, your church experience also includes many others, such as those in leadership.

From a child-raising point of view, the church is an extension of the home, not the other way around. In other words, a child's spiritual training begins at home, and the purpose of the church is to affirm that training. Remember, a parent should never look to the church as the primary spiritual teacher of the child. That is the job of the parent.

This is not to belittle the marvelous part a church can and should play in the upbringing of children. Your church creates the first stage of community outside the family in which children must learn to live. It provides your child with (one hopes) like-minded friends. It gives the parent a group of (one hopes) like-minded peers for counsel and support.

And, of course, the church undergirds the spiritual teaching of parents through its ministers, Sunday school teachers and youth leaders, as well as providing encouragement for all believers to worship the Lord. We cannot find this life-refreshing message anywhere else! This is why the Scriptures insist that we "not give up meeting together" (Hebrews 10:25).

All this goes upon the assumption that you and your church are spiritually in one accord, or at least in approximately the same place. It will do your child no good to hear you criticizing the church leadership—or even the Sunday sermon! A child sees the relationship between parents and their church as a natural extension of the relationship between the mother and the father. There are few things a child needs more than to know that the relationships around him are in harmony with one another.

WHY DO YOU GO TO YOUR CHURCH?

As silly as it may sound, this is a good question to ask yourself. Many people, when asked, respond by pointing out their churches' best points: the excellent sermons and teaching, the inspiring times of corporate worship, the various ministries, the love and friendships among the people. These are fine answers, and there are, of course, many others.

Suppose someone asks your children, "Why do you go to your church?" The vast majority will answer some variation of "Because that's where my parents go, of course." This is an acceptable answer. Indeed, it would be insane to have each child in your family try to pick out and attend his own church!

It is the parents' duty (not the child's) to select the church where the family will worship together. Nevertheless, just because the parents make the actual choice does *not* mean that they should select *their* favorite church. In other words, if the parents like a church because it meets their personal needs, but the children do not like it because it does not meet their needs, then perhaps that family is in the wrong church.

A Christian mother came to me for counsel about her rebellious teenage son. When I asked about the youth ministries in her church, she replied that they did not exist! When I suggested that they should find a church that had a dynamic youth group, she objected vigorously. "I love my church," she said. "The pastor gives wonderful sermons and I sing in the choir. I could never leave it."

I am sorry to say that the family is still in that church, and the son is more rebellious than ever. While this does not excuse his behavior, nor is it probably the only reason for his rebellion, it does point out the need for churches to have vibrant youth groups and for parents to put their children's needs *first*. If you have children and your church does not help in meeting their spiritual needs, then you may be in the wrong church—no matter how much you like it or how long you have attended.

Think of it this way. In the armed forces, the greatest generals have always held one belief in common: The needs of the common soldier always come first. Generals may order the soldiers into dangerous situations, but they give everything they can in the way of protection and comfort—often at their own discomfort. It is only inferior generals who care more for themselves than their soldiers' needs.

Great leaders have always put the needs of those in their care before their own needs. The ultimate example of this is, of course, our Lord Himself. Paul explains,

> Your attitude should be the same as that of Christ Jesus: who, being in very nature God, did not consider equality with God something to be grasped, but made himself nothing, taking the very nature of a servant being made in human likeness.
>
> PHILIPPIANS 2:5–7

To His own followers, Jesus said, "For even the Son of Man did not come to be served, but to serve, and to give his life as a ransom for many" (Mark 10:45).

So it should be in our families. And, frankly, you are an adult, a grown-up, a parent. If *your* needs are not being met in your church, you can always attend Bible studies, listen to tapes, read books and arrange for Christian fellowship. But your young children—in their critical formative years—have no such options. Their needs must come before yours. That is a price of good parenting. A powerful (and convicting) line from Thomas á Kempis' *The Imitation of Christ* bears remembering: "Wheresoever a man seeketh his own, there he falleth from love."

The local church can have a tremendous influence on your child's spiritual life and be a major encouragement to worship the Lord. Or it can create a prolonged period of resentment and frustration. It simply depends on which church you attend—one that majors in the all-important needs of its youth or one that does not. Choosing the right church becomes one of the most important decisions a parent can make. A later chapter will examine in detail the influence of your church's youth ministry.

Let us now look at one of the most essential instruments in the home environment for teaching children to worship: the family devotional.

5

Family Devotionals

Bring them up in the training and
instruction of the Lord.

EPHESIANS 6:4

A century ago it would not have been necessary to
write this chapter. In those bygone days, practically every Christian family had a daily event
known as the "family altar." The last half of the twentieth century witnessed an unfortunate decline in this excellent practice.
Today, if you ask people about a family altar, they will assume
that the local Christian bookstore is carrying some new piece of
furniture for the home.

It is worth noting that the last half of the twentieth century also witnessed a sharp rise in broken families, teenage rebellion and the abandoning of the Christian faith by millions of young people. Certainly, many factors contributed to these negative trends—they are not all due to the lack of the family altar! Yet the absence of a specific time of Christian fellowship and teaching is a prime factor in the breakdown of so many Christian homes because it is in the family where we communicate our highest values. Sir Winston Churchill reminds us: "There is no doubt that it is around the family and the home that all the greatest virtues, the most dominating virtues of human society, are created, strengthened and maintained."

Thus, I am glad to note that the family altar has not disappeared completely. Today we generally call this experience a "family devotional." Family devotionals are very important times for teaching children to worship God. They are so significant as to warrant an entire chapter on the subject. Indeed, if you do nothing else from this book except start a regular devotional time with your family, this volume will have a tremendous impact on you and your loved ones.

Different readers will have a variety of viewpoints on this subject: (1) Some have never tried it; (2) some have tried it only to fail (don't give up!); (3) others are working through family devotionals now, but need help; and (4) still others may have already discovered the great virtues of this practice and may appreciate new ideas. Wherever you are coming from, I urge you to consider prayerfully the principles given in this chapter.

To begin, we will look at family devotionals from the interrogatives: *what, why, when, where* and, most importantly, *how.*

WHAT EXACTLY IS A FAMILY DEVOTIONAL?

Rather than leave anyone behind, I will assume that this is a completely new concept for you. To answer the above question, let me first ask another by way of analogy: What is a family meal? (In these ultra-busy times, some people may not know what this is either!) Obviously, a family meal is a time when the members of a given family eat together.

Notice the many thousands of possible variations in a family meal. To begin with, the food will presumably vary day to day. The meal may be a massive Thanksgiving feast or it may be a quick bite. Someone in the family may not be present. At other times, friends or relatives may join in. Still other times will find a family at a restaurant or relaxing around a campfire. The only two factors that a family meal must contain are: (1) members of a family and (2) food. Everything else is quite flexible.

So it is with a family devotional. It is a time when *family members come together for spiritual encouragement.* It may be for Bible reading, but not always. It may include singing, but not always. Others may attend, and some members of the family may not be present. It may be long or short. In fact, like the family meal it will vary creatively from day to day.

The purpose is more important than the method. A family devotional is meant to bring parents and children together regularly for spiritual encouragement, just as attending church draws Christians from many families together regularly for spiritual encouragement. As every local church has its own "style," every family will as well. And as every church service mixes (mercifully!) variety with unity, so each family devotional should find a creative balance between these two extremes.

WHY ARE FAMILY DEVOTIONALS SO IMPORTANT FOR CHRISTIANS?

Consider God's timing: Did God create churches first or families first? Families, of course. They are the fundamental unit that God instituted with Adam, Eve and their children. As we saw in the preceding chapter, churches are a vital part of our faith, especially when we are raising children. But they can never take the place of the family itself.

Nevertheless, there are thousands of faithful Christian families who would not consider missing a Sunday service yet who never bother with regular family devotionals. This is absurd. It is like the man who buys a puppy and grooms it carefully but never remembers to feed it. He will soon have a well-groomed but dead dog. Likewise, without devotionals in your home, you may soon have a well-churched family but one that may be dying spiritually.

In the second chapter, we saw the essential need for modeling the Christian faith before our children. Frankly, it is a lot easier to look good in the church pew than in the home. If our children see us standing tall in church but constantly losing it at home, we may raise "churcheans" but not Christians. The great evangelist D. L. Moody once remarked: "A man ought to live so that everyone knows he is a Christian, and most of all, his *family* ought to know." It is in the home—with babies crying, toddlers wreaking havoc and teenagers grumbling—that our Christian modeling becomes paramount. This is when we teach our children that one can be a believer in the hard circumstances, not just the easy ones.

Devotionals are to the family what your church is to your Christian community. In both cases, you come together to worship, to pray, to examine God's Word, to serve and to encourage one another. Going to church will teach your children that you believe in weekly church attendance. Family devotionals will teach them that you believe in bringing your loved ones together to worship the Lord every day.

Admittedly, keeping family devotionals consistent and interesting can be an exhausting prospect to an already burned-out parent. I must confess that there have been days when it was time for our devotional and I groaned inwardly, "Not again. I'm too tired." Yet the fruit from our years of perseverance can be seen in the entire family. For in many ways, the family devotional is the modern equivalent of Jesus' actions in Luke 18:16–17:

> But Jesus called the children to him and said, "Let the little children come to me, and do not hinder them, for the Kingdom of God belongs to such as these. I tell you the truth, anyone who will not receive the Kingdom of God like a little child will never enter it."

The purpose of a family devotional is simple yet profound. The purpose is to *bring each member of your family (including yourself) closer to Christ every day*. That is why they exist. And that is why we need them so very much!

WHEN SHOULD YOU HAVE FAMILY DEVOTIONALS?

The purpose is, as we have seen, more important than the method. But if our methods are poor, we will never accomplish our purposes. Practical considerations, therefore, should be considered to ensure the highest quality and the greatest effectiveness.

Every family (and every family schedule) is different, so there is no one answer to the question When? The key word in your decision is *consistency*. That is, you must ask yourself, "When is the best time for family devotionals to enable them to be as consistent as possible?"

There is a great deal in the Bible about being consistent in our devotion to God. Yet some Christians will object: "We don't want to get *legalistic,* do we?" What they often label "legalism," however, the Bible calls "steadfastness" or "faithfulness." The Bible commends the man "who keeps his oath, even when it hurts" (Psalm 15:4). Yes, we are commanded to be very steadfast and faithful in carrying out our duties. Furthermore, the consistency you show in your family devotionals will demonstrate their importance to your children.

Some families find that early in the morning is their best time for devotionals. For others, it may be the last part of the day. Still others will link their devotionals to a certain meal, knowing that no matter how busy they are, they still have to eat! Again, the most important factor in choosing *when* is to consider how much it will help or hinder your staying consistent. Never forget the truth of Benjamin Disraeli's powerful words: "The secret of success is consistency of purpose."

We should also look at the related question How often? In a perfect situation, it would be best to have family devotionals every day, or at least Monday through Saturday, with your church's service representing the seventh day. Many families manage this, but others need a "day off" on Saturday. Remember that regularity is more important than frequency. It would be better to meet every Monday, Wednesday and Friday without fail, than to attempt to meet every day but only succeed once or twice each week.

Where Should You Have Family Devotionals?

Where is the best place for keeping family devotionals as consistent as possible? Around the dinner table? In the living room? On the back porch? Again, every family situation may dictate a different answer. (Moving occasionally can be helpful, adding variety.)

This critical factor cannot be ignored: *distractions.* Remember the old expression *prayer closet?* Not many of us go literally into our closets to pray (especially if your closet is as small and crowded as mine!), but the concept is a good one. We pray more effectively if we are in a place of few distractions.

In the same way, our family devotionals should take place where there is a minimum of distractions, particularly for the younger children. If your living room has a large aquarium that attracts the children's eyes, maybe this is not the optimal place for devotionals. If your dining room's picture window overlooks the neighbor's children playing, try another room. You do not have to be in a concrete-block cell, but find a place where everyone can concentrate.

Another important aspect deserving prayerful thought is the question How long? Many believers disagree on this subject; you, of course, know your children better than anyone else. A family devotional is *not* a Sunday church service! It is to be an enjoyable family time and appropriate to the age level of your children. Very few can handle a devotional longer than ten to fifteen minutes. This is not a new problem. Remember the youth in one of Paul's evening services that went a bit too long? "Seated in a window was a young man named Eutychus, who was sinking into a deep sleep as Paul talked on and on. When he was sound asleep, he fell to the ground from the third story and was picked up dead" (Acts 20:9). (The young man was revived by Paul, who, by the way, proceeded to talk until daylight!)

Some parents seem to feel as though God gives better marks for parenting according to the number of Bible verses crammed into their children's heads. Not true! Better to err on the shorter side, leaving the children happy and looking forward to further devotionals than have them bored and dreading tomorrow's tribulation. The leadership of our church's youth ministry has a meaningful saying: "It is a sin to bore a kid—even with a good message."

THE MOST IMPORTANT INTERROGATIVE: *How?*

Now we come to the crux of the matter: Exactly how should a parent conduct family devotionals? There are so many good answers to this question that we need to organize the possibilities. We will begin by looking at some general principles for every situation, and then plunge into specific ideas.

Positive Attitude. Children tend to take their cues from their parents. If you convey that you consider devotionals simply a duty, they will endure it as the same. If, on the other hand, you show that you are looking forward to the time, half the battle is already won. Ralph Waldo Emerson used to say, "Nothing great was ever achieved without enthusiasm," and it seems to be universally true. Keep in mind that family devotionals are always supposed to be enjoyable for everyone present, and this is essentially a *parental* responsibility.

Openness. We all want to be in a safe place where we can say anything and not be laughed at or criticized. I remember the night when one of our young sons said, "I believe that there are other gods, like fairies and nymphs." Thankfully, before his siblings could react (I nearly bit my tongue in half), my wife smiled and replied, "God has given you a wonderful imagination! Now let's see what the Bible has to say about that." Make certain that they know it is okay to bring up anything that is on their minds.

Variety. Whatever you choose from the "menus" given below, you should try to vary the recipe from night to night. You may love a great steak dinner, but not for every night of the month! In the same way, one devotional might emphasize Bible reading while another night could accentuate prayer for the missionaries you know. Variety keeps the children interested and the subjects alive.

"Serious Fun." Some people approach devotionals with solemn, long faces. Others seem to think that it is all fun and games. Perhaps a middle road is best, what might be called "serious fun." We never want to bore the children, but we do want to convey that mom and dad hold their Christianity with great devotion. We do not have to handle our Bibles with white gloves, but we do not throw them on the floor either. As in so many aspects of parenting, our challenge is to find the right balance. But it is imperative that our children see by example that their parents wholeheartedly love Jesus Christ and believe in the Word's final authority:

All Scripture is God-breathed and is useful for teaching, rebuking, correcting and training in righteousness, so that the man of God may be thoroughly equipped for every good work.

2 TIMOTHY 3:16–17

A word for parents who have older children and are just starting out with the idea of devotionals: Give a good deal of preparation time. Perhaps a week before your starting date, mention at dinner that you believe the family should have a short daily devotional time. Do not expect everyone to be thrilled! Explain calmly why you believe it to be important, and wait for it to settle in. Drop in other ideas during the week: "Perhaps we will read from Genesis or John." Let them get used to the idea.

Also strive to make the Scripture readings, discussions, etc. relevant to the ages of your children. Do you have a family with children of many ages? The rule of thumb is to lean toward the older children. If the older children think that devotionals are really for the little ones, they will be bored and set a poor example, which will be *very much* observed by the younger ones. Better to lose the younger ones occasionally than bore the older. Sometimes, if small children are present during a more "advanced" discussion, let them color to amuse themselves. In other words, if you have a four year old, a ten year old and a thirteen year old, your overall devotional should be geared toward the teenager, and the others will valiantly attempt to keep up—to be like the older ones.

Three Categories to Guide Your Devotionals

With these ideas in mind, let us now examine some of the many parts of a typical family devotional. To bring order to the possibilities, we will group them into three large categories: (1) the Bible, (2) prayer and (3) worship.

The Bible

I urge you to consider a modern translation when reading with your children. Personally I love to read the King James Version, but I would never ask my children to fathom such passages as "whithersoever thou goest" (Joshua 1:7). If you have very young children, read from a children's story Bible, available at most Christian bookstores.

Here are some ideas that readily lend themselves to a family devotional:

1. Read one book at a time, one chapter at each devotional. This gives order to the children's Bible knowledge, and you can let them choose the book to read (when this is age appropriate).

2. Read one chapter from the Old Testament, then one from the New (or alternate them from devotional to devotional). This teaches children the overall structure of our two-covenant Bible.

3. Choose endless variations on the above. You may want to read a short book (like Ruth) without interruption. For a longer one, such as Genesis, you may want to alternate with New Testament chapters or the Psalms.

4. Follow a published daily guide. Many fine ones are available, both in print and on the Internet.

5. Read randomly. Many Bible scholars are shocked by this suggestion, but there are times to bring it out from your repertoire of choices. You might begin by saying something like: "I'd like to read the fifty-third chapter of Isaiah today."

6. Choose biographies as your theme. Children love to read about such characters as Joseph, David, Esther and Paul. Don't forget the New Testament passages that refer to characters in the Old.

7. Follow a topical Bible study. This is particularly effective with older children. Do they know what the Bible says about generosity or humility or courage?

8. Study thematically. Sometimes it can be fascinating to "walk through the Bible" from Genesis to Revelation, finding passages that speak of one theme. These might include "God's Love for Us," "Making Right Decisions" or "Children and Parents."

9. Memorize a set of Bible verses. It is wonderfully bonding to memorize verses together with your family, especially if

they are related to a relevant topic. You can choose a set of verses yourself or use some of the excellent sets published by the Navigators ministry. Use different sets for children of varied ages (we created a "Toddler Memory System" for our preschoolers, with verses like "God is love" and "Jesus is Lord").

10. Memorize a chapter or a portion of Scripture together. This can also be very effective, particularly with older children. Short psalms (such as number 23 or number 100) or chapters (such as 1 Corinthians 13 or 1 John 1) are easy to handle. You might learn one verse each night. Perhaps the older children could aspire to the Sermon on the Mount (Matthew 5–7).

There are infinite variations of the above methods, so be creative. And remember to be sensitive to the different ages involved. With older children you can try for serious Scripture study while the younger ones play "Bible Baseball." Remember to resist the temptation to preach a sermon! Instead, allow time to ask questions and provoke interesting dialogue. Be sure to give time afterward for reflection and discussion or young minds may wander during the reading. Above all, consistent exposure to Scripture will teach the children a profound respect for the authority of God's Word.

Prayer

Family devotionals are a marvelous time for teaching our children to pray. Praying out loud in front of others who will not condemn them gives them confidence. Parents should always be aware that while they are praying to God, they are also setting an example for their children. A beautiful prayer to remember in this context is by British author Jane Austen: "Grant us grace, Almighty Father, so to pray as to deserve to be heard." In this case, we need extra grace since we are also heard by our impressionable children.

Here are a few ideas to consider as you incorporate prayer into your family devotionals:

1. Have all the children learn the Lord's Prayer and pray it together at devotionals occasionally. Not only is it a prayer in Jesus' own words, but it contains a great deal of teaching material that you can discuss with the family.
2. Pray "around the circle." That is, each of you prays, one at a time. The order should be announced beforehand. It could be by age or by seating.
3. If time is running out, ask one of the children to pray for the whole family. Remember not to ask the same one every time but to give this responsibility equally.
4. Select a specific *type* of prayer (such as thanksgiving, adoration, intercession) and ask each family member to use that type in the prayer time.
5. Select a certain topic or theme. These might include:

   A. Missionaries—either those you know personally or the missionary activities of specific countries.
   B. Your church—individuals in your local church, as well as pastors, elders and other leaders.
   C. Governmental leaders—the president, your senators and congressmen, governor, etc.
   D. Your relatives—those you see often as well as those you do not.
   E. Make up your own categories—always give your children opportunity for their input.

However you choose to give the example, the children need to learn to pray *in their own way.* This teaches them that they can

85

call upon the Lord in every circumstance, not just at family devotionals! A wonderful portrait of this is found in Acts 21:5, when
Paul was about to leave the believers at Tyre: "All the disciples
and their wives and children accompanied us out of the city, and
there on the beach we knelt to pray." One can easily visualize
the children praying devoutly, their knees deep in the sand. As
children make prayer a part of their daily lives, they invariably
deepen their personal relationship with the Lord.

Worship

As we have seen from the initial chapter of this book, both
Bible reading and praying are themselves a type of worship.
Indeed, *all* activities can become times of worship if our hearts
remain focused on the Lord. But now let us consider those
things that are more typically classified in most churches as
worship. This is usually centered around music and singing
but not exclusively so. Indeed, I encourage all parents to be
creative in family devotionals; some of the best ideas are found
in the realms of theater and the visual arts. Again, remember
that these ideas need to reflect your young children's interests
and abilities.

1. Rule one about singing: Be informed as to your children's
   favorite songs. Do not ask toddlers to attempt the typical
   Sunday worship songs, which many adults can barely
   handle! The best advice is: Sing the songs *they* want to
   sing. If it is not fun for them, try something else.
2. Whoever starts the song (presumably a parent), keep
   in mind the vocal range of your singers. Do not start so
   low that they are grumbling or so high that they are soon
   hyperventilating.
3. If there are instrumentalists in the family, encourage
   them to play for the family devotional. But remember

that many modern worship songs are quite difficult to play. It might be easier for the family if the singing is unaccompanied.

4. Unless your family is particularly musical, I do not recommend more than two or three songs in a family devotional. Keep in mind the essential word: *variety*. Remember that you do not have to imitate a Sunday morning church service.

5. For the younger children, try adding motions to the songs. They love them!

6. Drama can add a great touch to family devotionals. There are very few scenes in the Bible that our family has not acted out, usually with ridiculous props and lots of hilarity. Somehow, Dad always ends up playing the bad guy (or maybe the donkey that carried Jesus on Palm Sunday), and the kids alternate in the hero roles.

7. If your family is not the acting type, try dramatic readings. Many ministries publish short plays on the Web, often teaching important lessons.

8. How about worshiping with visual arts? Let each family member draw or paint a biblical scene or an abstract inspired by a Christian theme.

9. Try what might be called "waiting on God." After Bible reading and prayer, ask everyone to be silent and meditate on the Lord or on a certain Scripture. Do not "wait" too long with small children!

10. Always, always, always remember that family devotionals are meant to be *enjoyable*. Most children do well during Bible reading and prayer time. But many see worship as deeply personal and do not feel comfortable in public—even if the public is only their family. Pray for God to give you sensitivity about this. If they are not enjoying the worship time, then you are not teaching them how

to worship at all and may even be teaching them how to dislike worship!

Which leads to the next important point.

REACHING OLDER CHILDREN

Since this is a book about teaching children to worship, you are probably surprised that I have not made specific recommendations in this section on corporate worship *for older children*—those junior high age and up. Every family is different, of course, and you must discern what works best for your own. Nevertheless, I have seen outward worship completely turn off children to devotional time.

This is particularly true with singing. Young children love to sing and should be encouraged to do so. But when children near the junior high years, they become extremely self-conscious and easily embarrassed. Forcing them to sing along or enter into corporate worship can often spoil the good that the Bible reading and prayer have provided. Boys are perhaps worse than girls on this subject, but I caution you to be sensitive to the feelings of all your older children. As we will see in later chapters, there are other ways to encourage teenagers to worship—but not around their parents and younger siblings.

If in spite of your efforts your older children object to taking part in the family devotional time, tell them they must sit with the family, but that they may just listen quietly. Again, we are *not* talking about a long time. Any teenager can sit through a five- or ten-minute devotional, and it would set a dreadful example to the younger siblings if a teenager were allowed to be exempt.

If you still feel that you need more of a corporate worship experience with your older children, I recommend "breaking bread" together. Today we often think of a Communion service as formal and liturgical, but it is simply a commemoration of the Last Supper—and our Lord did say, "Do this in remembrance of me" (Luke 22:19). Teens generally feel more comfortable in this kind of service.

Again we must remind ourselves what a family devotional is truly about: It is a time when family members *come together for spiritual encouragement.* If what you are doing is not spiritually encouraging to your children (including teens) then try something else. If singing worship songs makes them uncomfortable or "feel like little kids," then do not sing worship songs! Instead, be content to immerse them in the equally important subjects of Bible reading, discussion and prayer.

A Few Examples of a Good Mix

For the sake of those readers who are new to this, I will give details for a few "sample" family devotionals. These are *not* to be followed ritualistically; they are only for the purpose of illustration. It is hoped that they will stir your own imagination to see the multitudinous possibilities and inspire you to seek the Lord for His direction in your unique devotional times.

Example One: A Short Devotional (5 Minutes)

1. *The Bible:* Read and comment upon a short passage of Scripture (2 to 3 minutes).
2. *Prayer:* Have each member of the family say a short prayer (2 to 3 minutes).

Example Two: A Moderate Devotional (15 Minutes)

1. *Prayer:* Ask each family member to say a prayer of thanksgiving for the many blessings in their lives (4 to 7 minutes).

89

2. *The Bible:* Read and discuss a passage from the Old Testament and another from the New (7 to 10 minutes).
3. *Prayer:* Say the Lord's Prayer together (1 minute).

Example Three: An Extended Devotional (30 Minutes)

1. *Worship:* Sing several songs of praise (4 to 5 minutes).
2. *Prayer:* Ask one of the family members to pray for God's blessing on your time together (1 minute).
3. *The Bible:* Have a short Bible study on the topic of overcoming fear (10 to 12 minutes).
4. *Prayer:* Have each member pray for different leaders in your local church (4 to 6 minutes).
5. *The Bible:* Review the Bible verses each member is memorizing (5 to 7 minutes).
6. *Prayer:* Close with a prayer of adoration (1 minute).

Earlier in this chapter I stated that the purpose of a family devotional is *to bring each member of your family (including yourself) closer to Christ every day.* This is what God intended from the beginning.

This purpose may not be fulfilled immediately, nor will every one of your family devotionals be spiritually supercharged. Teaching your children to worship God is a long-term project. Yet like the hundreds of bricks in a strong, well-constructed wall, the cumulative effect of a consistent devotional time is phenomenal. It helps to be reminded of the maxim by French poet Charles Baudelaire: "Nothing can be done except little by little." The little bits of time spent in family devotionals will give each member of your family the strength to stand and serve the Lord for life.

6

Your Child's Friends

There is a friend who sticks closer

than a brother.

PROVERBS 18:24

*W*hen we read the above verse, most of us smile with warm thoughts of a close friend. Perhaps we remember how a friend came to our rescue or shared a great laugh or stood by us in a painful time. Surely, it also inspires us to be steadfast friends to others.

But there is also a negative potential from those we call friends. They have influence over us, and it is not necessarily for good. From childhood onward, most of us have had friends who introduced us to all manner of trouble. Perhaps you will say, "Then they couldn't have been *real* friends!" True, but remember: We called them our friends at the time.

My best friend during several years of childhood was a boy named Greg. We played together for hours on end. But today I marvel at the times Greg talked me into doing some notorious pranks, often really hurting others. I feel ashamed knowing how I should have refused to take part in such mischief. But Greg was my friend, and in my immaturity I desired his approval.

In his outstanding book *The Four Loves,* C. S. Lewis discusses at great length the good and evil that friendship can promote. He points out that this wonderful gift called friendship, which can bring such delight and joy into our lives, can also turn us away from God. Friendship can both encourage Christians to stand up to persecution and be the binding camaraderie that keeps wicked men fighting through their last stand. Yes, even Hitler had friends.

My point? That as parents, we need to be *completely aware* of the friends who have gravitated toward our children, and vice versa, and take a proactive involvement in these friendships. Their potential—for good or ill—is stupendous. This is yet another extension of the biblical principle we will see throughout this book: "Know the condition of your flocks" (Proverbs 27:23). In chapter 3 we saw the importance of knowing your children. Now we expand this to knowing their friends.

A Gradual but Inexorable Process

A number of parents (particularly Christian parents) intend to be the number one influence on their children—with no close number two. Like mother hens, they watch over their broods with a jealous eye, making certain that nothing else comes too near. They are determined to be so wonderfully close to their children that any "non-family" influence will be insignificant.

They are dreaming. It is an elegant delusion, but a delusion nonetheless. You might as well attempt to hold back the ocean tide; you can try, but the waves will roll in without your permission. Normal, curious children will find ways around even the most protective parent. Unless you are grossly abusive (locking your children in closets, for instance) they are going to be greatly influenced by their friends—and probably sooner than you think.

To some degree, the relation between a child's two major influences, that of parents and friends, is inversely proportional. That is, as the influence of friends rises more and more, that of parents begins to wane. Parents have the greatest influence in the formative years, when the parent is virtually the child's entire universe. But as children begin to make friends, they gradually fall under their spell and begin to copy mannerisms, likes and dislikes, and habits. It is reasonable to expect that good parenting will always influence children, even after they have left home—it should never vanish entirely. But you are not in reality if you think that your child is not going to be strongly influenced by peers, perhaps more with every birthday.

When my wife and I became new parents, we presumed that "peer pressure" would probably not be an issue until our babies became teenagers. It was quite an eye-opener for us when our two year old came out of the church nursery one Sunday begging for a GI Joe T-shirt—because two other little boys had GI Joe T-shirts!

Over the years I have noticed hundreds of parents trying desperately to hold back the surging tide of peer influence. What we need, however, is not to shelter our children from peer influences. What we need is to direct our children to peers who *will be a good influence upon them*. If your son is suffering from breathing smog-filled air, the answer is not to tell him: "Don't breathe!" The answer is to get him to a place where there is *clean* air to breathe.

WHAT EXACTLY IS FRIENDSHIP?

Since most of us have had many friends throughout our lives, the above question may seem superfluous. But to be truly aware of the various degrees of friendship our children will encounter, we should start at the beginning. Most dictionaries include three basic ideas in their definitions of the word *friend:*

1. Someone you know well
2. Someone you like (presumably this is mutual)
3. Someone not in your family

Notice the difference in a relationship with an acquaintance or colleague, for whom only points one and three might apply. Friendship involves a deeper level of relationship.

Obviously, the closer the friends, the greater influence they will have upon our children. Parents do not need to worry themselves over the influence of every single classmate (unless they desire ulcers!). Yet those few individuals whom your children consider friends have a significant impact on their lives. These we need to know.

During the twenty or so years in their parents' care, most children will make hundreds of acquaintances, consider dozens of people friends and choose a handful of close friends. A healthy childhood will include friends of both sexes, but at this point, I am speaking of platonic friendship. Later we will consider the ramifications of deeper involvement with the opposite sex. At any rate, the parents' job is always to discern the strength of specific friendships in their children's lives and attempt to steer their children toward certain friends of good influence.

THE "DELEGATION" TOWARD INFLUENTIAL FRIENDS

There may be readers who object to the previous sentence, particularly the suggestion of giving direction: "Who am I to manipulate my child—who is after all an independent human being—into choosing certain friends while rejecting others? What arrogant coercion!"

Such parents should again read the introduction of this book, which demonstrates the undeniable duty of every Christian parent: to train his or her child about good and evil. Until young children are fully trained, parents have a duty to shelter them from evil. And this includes the potential evil that can result from the influence of the wrong friends. Cervantes reminds us: "Tell me thy company, and I'll tell thee what thou art." It is another way of stating Paul's essential principle of 1 Corinthians 15:33: "Do not be misled: 'Bad company corrupts good character.'"

This very week, as I am writing this chapter, I am attending a conference for the directors (and spouses) of many Christian ministries. Speaking confidentially with many of these couples, I have heard wonderful stories of grown children following the Lord as well as the heartbreaking stories of grown children who have rejected Christ. Without exception, every story of the heartbroken parents included a line such as, "Then he (or she) began to hang around with the wrong crowd."

As we determined earlier, you cannot keep your child from having friends. You can, however, select the friends your small children will play with. And as we will see later in this chapter, as children grow older you can help steer them toward positive influences. You see, when parents allow a friend to enter their young child's life, they are *delegating* the role of influence to that friend. This is a bit like delegating authority temporarily to a babysitter. When you send your child out the door to play with a friend, you are temporarily transferring the influence you have on your child to the friend. When we look at it in this light, we clearly see the importance of finding the right friends for such critical delegation.

Incidentally, the ability to direct our children toward the right friends is an imperfect one. You will sometimes be disappointed in the "good" friends you have tried to bring into your children's lives. (No matter how well you succeed, you will still need to pray!) But the wise parent is always aware of his or her child's close associates and never is guilty of simply looking the other way.

In many of the preceding paragraphs, you have read about finding "the right" friends for your young child. Before we consider how to go about this formidable task, let us first examine the actual quarry we are seeking. In other words, what are the qualities of a young friend who we believe would have the best possible influence on our children's lives?

KEY CHARACTERISTICS OF THE "RIGHT" FRIENDS

In order to encompass as broad a range of children as possible, I will keep these characteristics general. In other words, we will not be looking for friends with a specific lifestyle or talent-mix. Instead, we will look at five broad categories that are found in every society:

1. *A Love for God.* I am assuming (since you are reading this book) that you are a committed Christian. It should not surprise you, therefore, to find that the best friends for

your children would be children who love the Lord. They may be rich or poor, of any race, and come from a wide variety of denominational backgrounds, but if they have a heart for God, I recommend them as good friends for your child. When asked which was the greatest commandment, Jesus replied, "Love the Lord your God with all your heart and with all your soul and with all your mind" (Matthew 22:37). We need to look *actively* for other Christian children to play with our children.

2. *Good Relations with Their Own Parents.* This next category is a bit trickier. If you are able to connect your young children with other Christians, is that not enough? Actually, no, because traits are contagious. If a child who does not get along with his or her parents becomes close to your child, this negative characteristic could easily invade your own family. Good relations between parent and child are a must, ensuring communication through even the most difficult times. When chatting with one of my sons' new friends, I prayerfully try to discern about his family life. *The manner in which he answers* will often reveal if there is underlying rebellion against his parents.

3. *Kindhearted, Not Mean-Spirited.* This seemingly obvious category has to do with the vulnerability of children, in this case, your children. Although kids will sometimes complain about a mean teacher or a tough coach, the people who can hurt them the most are often their own age. Ask any adult about painful childhood memories and you will find just how cruel one child can be toward another. Be on your guard, therefore, if your child gravitates toward someone you can see is mean-spirited. He or she may extend friendship toward your child for a while, but it may be only a matter of time before a painful situation arises.

97

4. *Fun-Loving.* It is only natural that your child wants *to have fun* with his friends. If you only push him or her toward the dullest kids you can find, you will receive some well-deserved resistance. Children need to hear that their parents want them to be happy—not just down the road in their ultra-responsible future, but today! A healthy child will never be inspired by a message such as, "I never had fun when I was a kid, and you're not going to either." Instead, encourage him to have a great time when at play, and find friends who will complement this contagious attitude.

5. *A Desire to Excel.* Some children are naturally inclined to improve themselves, while others seem content to vegetate in front of the TV. Granted, those who desire to excel tend to make good grades, but do not simply look for perfect report cards. They also want to succeed in all areas of life and improve in those particular areas in which they are talented and motivated. These "self-starters" can have a fantastic influence on your children, helping them discover their unknown talents and giving them the confidence to excel. Begin teaching the principle of Proverbs 22:29 at an early age: "Do you see a man skilled in his work? He will serve before kings; he will not serve before obscure men."

Lots of kids fit in all the above categories! Your church is probably full of them. And if you cannot find any right away, start praying regularly that God will bring the right friends for your children.

DIRECTING YOUR OLDER CHILD TOWARD THE RIGHT FRIENDS

If you are a boss of a small company and want the best employees, then you hire very carefully. After selecting the finest available, you train them. If someone is hired who should not have been, someone who steadfastly refuses your efforts at training, then you have the option of firing him or her.

Not so with your older child's chosen friends. You cannot fire them. Emerson spoke truly when he said: "We can force no doors in friendship." This applies to opening and closing doors. If certain friends really are a bad influence, you might forbid your child from seeing them. But this often produces rebellion and should only be invoked as a last resort. Two other methods should always be attempted first.

The first might be called a "posture of disapproval." That is, if you notice a friendship emerging that you feel is not a good influence, you should *subtly* make your child aware of your lack of enthusiasm. No arguments. No threats. You might say (with no emotion) something like, "You know, I'm a bit concerned about (name)." When your child asks for details, remain calm and vague: "I'm not sure I'd want him for a close friend."

Leave it there. Too much complaining will often encourage your child to begin defending the friend, thus increasing his loyalty to him (or her). This subtle approach should be tried first. Remember Proverbs 25:15 can apply to anyone: "Through patience a ruler can be persuaded, and a *gentle* tongue can break a bone" (emphasis added). You have indicated your disapproval and it may be enough to caution your child not to become close to this person. At any rate, it is always wise to withhold the "big guns" of parental authority until they are truly needed.

The second approach is quite practical, especially with preteens. Since the parent is in control (we assume) of the family's weekly schedule—as well as the family car—you can encourage good friendships and avoid bad ones with simple decisions. When children who are a good influence want to come over, you are happy and able to pick them up (whatever sacrifice it takes) and drive them home. But when children who are a bad influence want the same, you are not so accommodating. I am certainly not advocating that you lie; rather, I am suggesting that you "go the extra mile" to bring good influences into your child's life.

There will be moments when you must talk to your child openly about the negative influence of a certain friend. This is one of the most delicate times of parenting. I do not recommend the blunt command, "Don't hang around (name) anymore!" It may give you the illusion of strong leadership, but it will often challenge your child to want to hang around (name) even more so. A sensitive, non-threatening conversation will explain why you are so concerned. Again, your child may not agree with your reasoning, but she will be assured that you have her best interests at heart.

At this point, someone might object, "You're concerned about the influence my children's friends have on them. What about my children's influence on *their* friends?" Of course you desire that your children will be a good influence on others. This will happen naturally if they possess the five traits outlined above. As we have already seen in previous chapters, parents should be modeling such virtues at home every day. The point of this chapter is to ensure the continuing growth of such virtues. Thus, a child's life must include certain friends and avoid certain others.

Same Church, Different Standards!

As you can imagine, the obvious place to find potential friends for your child is in your local church. Presumably you would not be there if you did not agree with its basic teaching, so your church can become an excellent resource for finding like-minded families. Depending upon the size of the church, you may have a wealth of children around you who already possess the same type of fundamental training you are giving your own child.

Nevertheless, new parents be warned: Simply going to a good church with many children does not solve all your problems. Within every church are dozens of families who probably disagree on a myriad of issues. We may all read the same Bible and hear the same sermons but we do not agree on every aspect of parenting! And this causes many problems in the local church. Few of us have learned to accept one another "without passing judgment on disputable matters" (Romans 14:1).

Movies are a prime example. Hollywood has such a habit of sullying even the cleanest topics that many families are constantly trying to decide if next week's blockbuster is appropriate for their children. You may decide that you do not want that trash in your home—only to find out that the pastor's kids love that movie! Or your child's friends come to your house and watch a movie that you consider acceptable—only to have their parents treat you like a pariah who has corrupted their children!

Dozens of similar issues are debated by sincere Christian parents within the same church. TV, clothes, entertainment and music are just a few topics that can become paramount to your children and extremely contentious in the Body of Christ. I know of people who have left churches, not because of doctrine, but because the youth group endorsed certain styles of music.

What is a parent to do? As usual, the first thing you should do is pray, and the second is to talk with your children. You have to explain that each family has its own standards on many issues. Explain what your family's standards are on such and such an issue, but point out (without *any* condemnation) that other families in your church feel differently—and that you need to respect their decisions.

Our children need to learn this principle at an early age, that many times people have to "agree to disagree" and still love one another. Indeed, if we are going to raise worshiping children, then they must learn to worship the Lord with people with whom they may disagree on a number of subjects. In fact, each of us does so every Sunday morning!

Speaking of "agreeing to disagree," let us examine an important topic that has Christian parents everywhere weighing the pros and cons: Where should my children go to school?

Public School, Christian School or Homeschool?

This question is one of the most difficult to answer for today's Christian parent. It is also one of the most controversial, since many Christians believe that only one of them (take your choice) is the correct answer, and therefore the other two (take your choice) are completely incorrect. As this chapter concerns the all-important topic of your child's friends, and the parent's decision regarding schooling will determine where many of those friends are, we must deal with this question forthrightly.

If you ask Christian parents who have made the decision about where to send their children to school, they will tell you all about *the good* that came from their choice. This is, of course, a form of self-justification. That is, we make a difficult or insecure choice, and then—in order to feel better about this choice—tell others (and ourselves) what a good choice it was. This can quickly lead to criticizing the choices made by other Christians.

As someone who has spent years involved with all three of these educational methods, I want to tell you something you do not often hear: There are also *problems* with *each* of these methods. None of them will solve all your educational and parental issues. Each has advantages and disadvantages, and we would do well to admit it.

No one else can tell you which is best for your family. They are not the shepherd of the sheep (see John 10:11). *You* are. Only you will have to answer before God about how you reared your children. Let us make one thing quite certain: Children who love to worship God can (and do) come from all three systems, and children who fall away from the faith also can (and do) come from all three systems. So each parent needs to seek the Lord prayerfully in making this important choice. In fact, various children from the same family may need to be in different educational systems.

Obviously, this choice has a great deal to do with the friends your child will make. If your child is in a public school, you will want to search out other Christian families there. If you opt for a Christian school, you should still be aware that this does not guarantee perfect Christian students in every classroom. And if you decide to homeschool, you may need to make special efforts (probably extra driving) to ensure that your children have healthy contact with believing friends.

Whatever educational choice you make, do not make the terrible mistake of condemning other Christian families who make different choices—especially in front of your children! Some parents will say (harmlessly, they imagine), "We love you so much as to make *this* choice." This implies to your child that those other parents do not love their children as much—a horrible teaching. Later, as your child learns that those parents do indeed love their children, the validity of your education method (and your integrity!) will be questioned.

An excellent verse to remember in such controversial matters is Romans 14:22: "So whatever you believe about these things keep between yourself and God." Comparing your family to others in front of the children is the fastest way to encourage them to be judgmental of other believers. They do not need this, and neither does the Body of Christ. Instead, as with the issues of different music or movie standards, say something like, "God calls different families to do different things. This is what we believe He wants us to do. What the other families do is none of our business."

THE INEVITABLE WORLD OF BOYFRIENDS AND GIRLFRIENDS

Moving from one controversial area to another, we now enter the intrepid realm of friends of the opposite sex. By this I do not mean the innocent platonic relationships that should happen between the sexes at almost any age. There is nothing controversial there. But when your children pass through adolescence and the greater passions begin to rise, we have a new type of "friend influence" to deal with—and there are many conflicting teachings about this in the Church today.

Entire books have been written on this subject; I will deal with it only as it pertains to raising worshipful children. Indeed, certain aspects of this new time of parenting can actually encourage your children in worship. God often uses a young person of the opposite sex to inspire your child—in a healthy, non-sexual manner—to come closer to Christ. This is doubtless within His will, and we should be careful not to deter it, even as we are diligent to teach our children the supreme virtues of purity and holiness.

The first point that must be made concerning this subject has to do with timing. It might be called "not too soon." Hollywood has our pre-adolescent children already thinking about boyfriends and girlfriends when they should be playing ball and doing youthful chores. As we shall see further in the final chapter, timing is very important. You do not demand an eight year old to worship as an adult or as a teenager would. Similarly, you do not encourage romantic relationships at an unnaturally young age.

A correlation to this topic has to do with music—yes, even "Christian music." As adolescence blooms and the hormones kick in, your child will generally gravitate toward "heavier" (usually louder!) music. This is quite common, and we can be grateful that some excellent Christian bands give alternatives to the unhealthy secular versions. But try to hold this urge back in younger children. It will be a problem later (what will they listen to *then!*) if your younger ones have already graduated from VeggieTale songs to Christian hard rock.

The most significant factor of these romantic, hormonally charged times is again one of *influence*. Some parents, trying desperately to ensure purity, have practically cut off their teenage children from any contact with the opposite sex. In doing this, they may have inadvertently discouraged relationships with devoted worshipers who could have been a wonderful influence on their children. If parents have spent years teaching children biblical principles—especially that of *never* having romantic relations with an unbeliever—then the teenage years and the friends they bring can prepare children to form a faith that will truly be their own, and not merely that of their parents.

Of course, this does not mean that if your teenager happens to be attracted to a strong Christian you can leave them to their own devices! The hormones are still surging, and consistent teaching (and alertness on the parent's part) is absolutely needed. An excellent practice to encourage is that of "mixed groups." Instead of spending hours alone in a romantic relationship, they can both spend time together in small groups of friends. You may feel that such peer groups do not provide the best accountability. Compared to the temptations resulting from a young couple being alone, however, small groups can solve a great deal of teenage relationship problems.

IS THE PARENT'S DUTY EVER FINISHED?

Here is yet one more issue on which church leaders will disagree. Some will say that at 18 or at 21 or when your child is "on his own" your job has ceased. Others say this happens on the day of his marriage. Still others hold out for the day of the parent's death!

Rather than see parental responsibility as having an on-off switch, perhaps it would be better to note how, in a healthy relationship, our positions gradually modify. As we nurture our infants, we are everything in their worlds. With our youngsters, we encourage friendships with children we have selected. As parents of teenagers, we watch out for negative influences, while steering them toward positive ones. With our college students, we write letters and e-mails, giving our offspring freedom—but with a strong dose of parental advice. Even after they marry we retain bonds of love, being always prepared to offer (but never insist upon) our counsel.

If there is any one aspect of parenting that should never change, even if we live to attend our child's one-hundredth birthday party, it is prayer. This is particularly true regarding the influence of friends upon your children. Never forget Paul's words: "With this in mind, be alert and always keep on praying" (Ephesians 6:18). When they are in our homes, we model the Christian walk and involve them in worship as is appropriate to their ages. But as they walk out the door and into the influence of others, our prayers must affect what our physical presence cannot.

7

Home-Life Principles
That Encourage Worship

Sons are a heritage from the LORD, chil-
dren a reward from him.

PSALM 127:3

This chapter may be the most important for many
readers. It offers ten parenting principles selected
specifically because of their direct connection to
teaching worship. That is, these principles, when lived out consistently by parents, will encourage a lifestyle of worship.

The following ideas are not in any particular order and they
do not build toward a dramatic climax. Each heading, and the

information that follows, offers a principle that parents might want to consider implementing in their homes. As you read, do not simply contemplate how this might apply to your family *today*. Consider the effect that years of such practices will have on leading your children into a permanent state of adoration for their Savior.

Teaching your children to worship is not a short-term project. We must always be looking for ways to express parental love, which is the closest expression we have of the true love that flows from the Lord. Ultimately, this is the goal of these principles—that our actions may encourage our children to discover, then appreciate, then respond to the ever-present love of God.

EXPRESS GRATITUDE FOR YOUR CHILDREN

Adults typically relate to God in the way they learned as children to relate to their parents. Perhaps the most basic example has to do with the conception of our children: Are we happy or unhappy that our children are here? Do they see this in our speech and actions? Do we consistently demonstrate the supreme gratitude we feel about having them in our family?

Hmmm. This can be a painful area for some. Perhaps your child resulted from an "accident." Perhaps you were disappointed or even terrified when you first learned that a baby was coming. Perhaps the pregnancy was filled with pain and anxiety, and the memory of it causes you to wince in anguish.

Whatever the circumstances surrounding the conception of your children, that is in the past and we must endeavor to leave it there. It is an extremely important parental duty to convince our children that we were delighted at their arrival. They need to hear this, to know that they were (and are and always will be) *wanted*.

For, of course, if we believe Scripture, then there are really no such accidents. As God declared to the prophet Jeremiah, "Before I formed you in the womb I knew you" (Jeremiah 1:5). Nevertheless, we can easily be distracted from this reality and communicate our error to our children. Indeed, if at times you feel less than grateful for your children, then you had better play the actor. That is right, pretend—for their sake.

Our children need to hear such statements as, "We were *so* excited when you were born" and "The best gift God has ever given me was you children" and "Being a parent is the greatest thing that has ever happened to me," etc., etc. Comments like "Why did we have all these kids, anyway?" or "I think we had better give some of them back" or "We were so surprised when you came along" can do more damage than we realize. As English philosopher John Locke remarked, "Parents wonder why streams are bitter when they themselves have poisoned the fountain."

It is difficult to worship God if you are unsure of His love. In order not to hinder our children's future worship of the Lord, we must emphasize the biblical truth that God loves them unconditionally. And the best way for us to teach this truth is to show that we, as their parents, love them unconditionally. We need to model the picture of God's love for us found in Scripture: "He will take great delight in you, he will quiet you with his love, he will rejoice over you with singing" (Zephaniah 3:17).

BE HUMBLE AND ASK FOR FORGIVENESS

A typical scenario: You have had a bad day at the office, still smarting from missed deadlines, obnoxious coworkers and a host of other problems. You come home to a house of noisy children and an equally exhausted spouse who, instead of ministering to your pain, needs your help. Over dinner the two teenagers start arguing and you finally lose it, exploding in a harmful—if understandable—tirade of anger and frustration.

Now what? You blew it, and you know you should not have, since "good parents" never scream at their children, right? Well, this is the real world, and it happens. The big question now is: What are you going to do about it?

In many households, such situations are never truly resolved. Instead, the children know that they had better stay away from whichever parent exploded and that eventually things will calm down, at least until the next time. Yet the Bible points to a better solution. Sooner or later, the parent needs to say something like this to the family: "I owe you all an apology. I'm deeply sorry I exploded at the dinner table. I was wrong to do so and I ask for your forgiveness."

Such a humble sentiment results in reconciliation and renewed relationship. Yet it is so seldom employed. Why? Because there is a part of us that simply cannot stand to utter those three little words: *I was wrong.* We would rather make excuses or blame others. For men, in particular, our pride tells us that we will appear weak if we say such a humbling statement. Yet it is to this we are called.

I wish I could honestly tell you that I always make such an apology when needed. It would be untrue. But I will say this: Whenever I do talk myself into doing the right thing and ask forgiveness from my children, it produces a closeness that is absolutely beautiful. Far from appearing weak to them, I find that I receive a huge amount of respect that would not have been gained without the apology.

But there is still a further benefit, and it has to do with teaching worship. When a parent sincerely apologizes and asks forgiveness, he or she demonstrates to the child that even parents are not above the law. That is, we show that there is a higher authority, and that we "also have a Master in heaven" (Colossians 4:1). Our public submission to that Master and His law is yet another proof that we consider Him worthy of our worship. Such humbling can be a tremendous encouragement for children to worship this Master who is above all worldly authority—even parents.

BE SURE THAT DAD (NOT JUST MOM) LEADS SPIRITUALLY

One does not have to be a trained psychologist to realize that there are fundamental differences between masculinity and femininity. Yes, men in general have a difficult time with actions like apologies. Other areas are also quite tricky for us, and one is spiritual leadership in our families.

Many have speculated as to why this is such a common problem, one that is manifested in a number of ways. Look around any church congregation. You will notice more women than men. You will also notice a number of families without a father present. Of course, in some cases the father has died or is ill, but that is the exception rather than the rule. Dennis Rainey, an expert writer on Christian families, sums up the problem for us: "The breakup of the family isn't due to a deterioration in our legislators' values, but rather to a deterioration in fathers' values."

When a father allows his wife to be the prominent spiritual force in the family, it can have formidable long-term effects on the children. For the sons, it proclaims that Christianity is really for the females, so you do not have to take it seriously. For the daughters, it damages the important portrait of the father heart of God, which may later produce insecurities about God's love for them. It both cases, it demonstrates a lack of oneness that should emanate from the household's leadership.

This, of course, does *not* mean that the mother should have nothing to do with the spiritual leadership of a family. Abusing a mother by ignoring or demeaning her spiritual input can have devastating effects on the children. The solution to one error is not to embrace the contrary extreme.

A balanced approach is surely the best answer. In such areas as family prayer or devotional time, both parents need to be solidly involved. This offers role models for both boys and girls. Furthermore, it demonstrates that mom and dad are spiritually in one accord. This is one of the most significant ingredients in inspiring your children to worship God: seeing the ways of the Lord reflected in their parents' lives.

LEARN TO HANDLE DISAGREEMENTS AT THE TOP

As you might imagine, the Bible does not give us an example of members of the Trinity working out a disagreement! This is not needed in the perfect unity of the Divine, but for a typical husband and wife, it certainly is. No two people, no matter how in love or how spiritually mature, will agree on everything and they may often disagree on extremely important issues of child rearing. The *manner* in which they resolve their differences can be either a beautiful teaching to the children or a deplorable example to be repeated in future generations.

Shelves could be filled with books on marital conflict resolution. We will not resolve all of them here. The aspect of this subject that pertains the most to the teaching of worshipful children is threefold: (1) self-control, (2) privacy and (3) resolution.

1. *Self-Control.* When a troubling disagreement erupts in public (for instance, at the dinner table), the first duty of a Christian couple is self-control—an essential virtue commended throughout Scripture (see Titus 2:2, 5–6). They must immediately put the brakes on the feelings of anger and curb their tongues from lashing out. This does

not mean a permanent suppression, but a temporary truce until an appropriate time and place (the sooner the better) can be found for resolution. The demonstration of self-control in potentially volatile situations can in itself be a powerful teaching for your children to emulate.

2. *Privacy.* It must be emphasized that resolving arguments can best be accomplished without an audience, especially an audience of children. Paul tells us that when there is quarreling about words, it "ruins those who listen" (2 Timothy 2:14). Mom and dad should go to a room by themselves and keep their voices down as they work through the disagreement. Again, self-control is needed in order to avoid making painful verbal attacks that will be slow in healing. Instead, each party needs to calm himself and pray for understanding.

3. *Resolution.* Problems and disagreements should never be allowed to fester but should be resolved as soon as possible. The Scriptures command us: "Do not let the sun go down while you are still angry" (Ephesians 4:26). When things have calmed down and both parties have asked for and received forgiveness, then mom and dad should rejoin the rest of the family. The children do not need to hear details, but they do need to realize that the parents are in one accord again. Of course, some problems will take longer than this to resolve, but the process should be started immediately. Knowing that problems can and will be resolved contributes to the feeling of stability in the children, and will give them security to rely on God's steadfastness.

Uphold Other Authorities Before Your Children

We now need to consider the other authorities in your child's life: teachers, coaches, youth group leaders, police officers, politicians, etc. If you think about it, you will realize that worship has a great deal to do with the concept of authority. For example, you can never really worship God until you are quite happy with and grateful for His authority over you. Without this understanding, the relationship between you and God is out of order.

With this in mind, we need to give our children a healthy picture of all true authorities—not only their parents but all others who will come into their lives. Children must find that these authorities are their friends, not their enemies, and that they have been placed here by God Himself. "The authorities that exist have been established by God" (Romans 13:1). They should learn how to make a respectful appeal and to submit to the authority's judgment even if they disagree with the outcome.

Consider, for instance, how you speak about your child's teachers at the dinner table. If you complain about them or degrade them in any way, you are destroying not only your own authority in the eyes of the child but God's as well. Young children in particular tend to view all authorities as a whole, and the idea that mom's authority is good but the teacher's is bad makes little sense to them. If they are not to obey the teacher, they may soon begin to wonder why they should obey mom.

Most children notice their parents' reactions to all authorities and mimic our example (for good or ill). This is common to every household. Do they hear you complaining about your boss, disagreeing with your pastor or mocking the politicians who serve us? If so, we may be planting the wrong seeds.

You may say, "What if a local politician is obviously corrupt? Do I praise him in front of my child?" Of course not. But you must show him *respect* in front of the child. Even if you abhor the mayor or governor or president, you must demonstrate respect *for his position*. Remember, the apostle Paul lived during the time of the notorious Emperor Nero, but his letters offer no complaints; rather, they call for respect and submission to every position of authority—as long as the believer is not put into a position of sin against God's law.

Always keep in mind the long-term consequences of our modeling before our children. Today, they may laugh with you if you make fun of a teacher or politician. Tomorrow, they may make fun of you. Instead, let them follow your example of respect for your authorities. This will transfer to their respect for God's authority—without which there will be no worship.

WATCH THE WAY YOU TALK
ABOUT YOUR CHILDHOOD

Every reader of this book will, of course, have a different background. I cannot know whether your parents were kind and loving or cruel and malevolent. But whatever our memories about our upbringing, the manner in which we talk to our children about them is worthy of our attention.

Consider these differences. One parent tells the children, "I had a wonderful time in school and I want to make sure you have a wonderful time as well." Another parent says, "When I went to school, I had to walk ten miles, often in the rain or snow, and I was grateful!" (The children roll their eyes.)

Most of us have a combination of positive memories and negative memories—some of which might be best forgotten. The least we can do for our children is not to rub our negative memories in their faces. This does not mean lying to them. It does mean using discretion, lest we accidentally condemn our children to repeat our mistakes and heartaches.

This is particularly true if the parents were not raised as believers. I cringe whenever I hear parents give "testimony" to the horribly sinful teenagers they were before accepting Christ. What they are subtly teaching their children is that they, too, can be horrible sinners in their teens—don't worry, there will be plenty of time to repent later! When the apostle Paul mentions the pre-conversion life, he describes it as "the things you are now ashamed of" (Romans 6:21). Why should we want to dwell on such things, if indeed we are ashamed of them as we ought to be?

Years ago, as the principal of a Christian school, I had one student who was always on the edge of failure. We tried everything (unsuccessfully) to help this boy, who was not rebellious and seemed of average intelligence. In a conference with his father, I asked about his own schooling. He answered, "I hated school and was always flunking. But I tell my kid, you've got to do better than I did!" The problem was quite obvious.

Most children will, sooner or later, try some of the same tricks you have reported. "Why shouldn't I?" they argue. "You did when you were my age!" It will avail you little to answer with the excuse, "Well, you have better teaching than I did." It would have been better never to have revealed your erring past. It has been forgiven and forgotten by the Lord; perhaps you had better forget it yourself.

Many adults are still without Christian victory because they are hanging onto past guilt rather than accepting with faith our forgiveness in Christ. This dwelling upon past sins spills over into their parenting, and gives children the hideous theology of "incomplete forgiveness." Alexander MacLaren, the greatest British preacher of the early twentieth century, told his congregation: "Forget your past circumstances, whether they be sorrows or joys. The one is not without remedy, the other not perfect. Both are past; why remember them? Why should you carry about parched corn when you dwell among fields white for harvest?"

Some parents may object to the prudence I am counseling, asking, "Why should I hide from my children who I really was?" Because a parent's responsibility is always to consider how such revelations may affect the child. Remember that a child's basic instinct is to imitate his parents, both their good and bad actions. Almost all of us have at least some good memories from childhood, and these should be told and retold. By emphasizing the positive over the negative, we will give our children a greater chance to embrace the good times in their own lives. It will also enable them to worship the Lord with greater freedom than you may have encountered as a child.

TAKE VACATIONS

Everyone loves vacations, or so we are told. So why are so few of us taking them? Granted, the Bible calls us to work hard and to provide for our families, and it is usually difficult for many families to get away. Nevertheless, a vacation is to a family year what a Sabbath is to a family week, a beautiful and memorable time for true bonding to take place.

Two typical excuses for a curtailing of family vacations are money and time, or rather the lack of money and time. As to the former, I can easily sympathize. Our family vacations are not exactly world tours. But we have found that the children enjoy a cheap camping trip just as much as a week at Disney World. What they are really after is an extended time when both mom and dad are completely theirs, without the distractions from household and office. This is why pocket pagers and laptop computers are the kiss of death to a family vacation.

As to the second common excuse, a lack of time, I sometimes think we parents need to be completely honest with ourselves. Most adults get a great deal of self-esteem from our work, no matter how much we complain about it. The subconscious tries to tell us: "If I can get away from the office so easily, then maybe I am not really important there after all." So we keep ourselves busy and call ourselves hard workers or good providers. Meanwhile, the true provision *of our time* with our children is squandered—and they grow up all too quickly.

Vacations are more than simply fun and games (though we could all use a bit more of this, too). These are the times when memories are created. These are the times when children can really get to know their parents. These are the times when, without the distractions of TV and school friends, the only moral influences are coming directly from the parents.

God commanded the Jews to come together with their entire families for festival celebrations three times each year (see Exodus 23:14) so that they might worship Him. I cannot help but believe that He had another purpose in mind as well: to bring the families together on a kind of "enforced vacation," taking them away from their daily duties and giving them quality time with one another.

For this very reason, I strongly recommend that, if at all possible, you spend your vacation times *away* from your home. Sometimes parents will decide to stay home, usually to save money. "Don't worry, kids," they announce. "We're still going to play lots of games and have a great time." Maybe this will happen, but the home is filled with many familiar distractions to tempt us away from pure family time. Contrast this with a camping trip, sitting around a campfire with nothing to do but be a family together. No phone, no TV, no neighborhood friends, just you and your children. If camping does not suit your family, plan trips to a park, a beach or a museum.

Family devotionals during vacations can be quite meaningful, though please be sensitive to your children's needs during this special time. Since they are probably "straining at the bit" to start having fun, they may groan when they see you pulling out a Bible—especially if the devotional times are too long. Announce your plans for devotionals beforehand, and keep them short. Rather than resenting this time, the children may find the memory of reading God's Word by firelight one they will never forget.

MAINTAIN PERSONAL STANDARDS

In the second chapter, we looked at a concept called the Modeling Principle. It states that *we cannot expect our children to be any more dedicated to Christ than we are ourselves.* Being dedicated to Christ is, of course, a spiritual condition that cannot be measured quantitatively. Yet our children take notice of how our personal lives relate to our Christian dedication. D. L. Moody knew the significant impact a Christian's morals can have on those around him. "Where one man reads the Bible," he pointed out, "a hundred read you and me."

James asks, "What good is it, my brothers, if a man claims to have faith but has no deeds?" (James 2:14). Obviously, our deeds cannot merit us salvation, but they are the *evidence* of our faith, the natural outgrowth of our spiritual walk. Children need to see such evidence, which proves to them that our actions at home are congruent with the faith we speak.

A modern rendition of James' question might be: "What good is it, my brothers, if a man claims to have faith but watches trashy movies or reads pornographic magazines or books?" From our children's point of view, we could rephrase the question this way: "What good is it, my parents, to tell me of your faith in God (and expect me to have the same faith), if you do not practice what you preach?" Even if we *tell* our children that the Bible is our ultimate authority, they will not truly believe us unless we *do* what it says.

According to many teenagers, hypocrisy is one of the principal excuses for abandoning the faith of their parents. By this they mean that our "walk" does not equal our "talk." In 1 Corinthians 4, Paul speaks of his "way of life in Christ Jesus" (that is, his lifestyle), and then adds an important note: "which agrees with what I teach" (1 Corinthians 4:17). It is this agreement that our children are looking for. It will enable them to follow our example and worship our God.

Take a look around your home. Do you see books or movies that would embarrass you if your pastor dropped in unexpectedly? If so, realize that your children have noticed them as well, and they recognize the incongruity between these items and teaching about the purity of the Gospel. Some items may fall within the permissible range of our Christian freedom, yet they can be stumbling blocks for our children. If in doubt, err on the side of caution. Give your children an illustration of "clean hands and a pure heart" (Psalm 24:4).

STRIVE TO MAKE YOUR CHILDREN *PROUD* OF YOU

That's right, *proud* of you. Such a word may bring objections from those faithful believers who have rightly spent their lives trying to flee from any form of pride. Yet the Bible gives us this picture of a godly family: "Parents are the pride of their children" (Proverbs 17:6).

This passage of God's Word suggests that if our children are *not* proud of their parents, something is wrong. Of course, the problem may come from either side. As noted in the introduction to this book, each child is ultimately a free agent and can decide to rebel despite our best efforts. In other words, when there is a problem between you and your child, the fault may lie with you, with the child or with both of you—probably the most common scenario. One of our jobs as parents is to examine our own lives and remove anything that gives a poor example to our children.

Children have an inborn desire to be proud of their parents. This may surprise you if you have watched Hollywood's many portrayals of families in the last few decades. Parents (especially dads) are foolish, stupid, geeky, cowardly, selfish and only competent at embarrassing their children. Yet the proclamation of most youngsters—"My dad can beat up your dad"—still resonates within them.

As we examine the behavior we habitually display before our children, we need to consider how we act toward them *in front of their friends*. For some strange reason, more parents than we might expect (parents who are normally kind to their children in private) show another side when their young friends are present. They become complainers, finding fault with their children and belittling their interests. How do the children feel about this public humiliation? We might gauge it with this question: Do my children want to bring their friends to *our* house, or would they rather be at their friends' houses?

The solution to this problem is not complicated: We simply take a friendly, sincere interest in our children's friends, not trying to be a "cool" young person (we will not succeed in this anyway) but simply an enthusiastic parent. When you meet these young friends, smile and greet them warmly. Thank them for coming to your home. Ask about their families and interests. Avoid saying anything that might embarrass your child.

You do not have to be a notable public figure for your children to be proud of you in the biblical sense. It will come naturally if you are simply sensitive to them and their needs. As they develop pride in their parents, they will learn to be proud of the God who loves them. This will encourage them to share their faith in this wonderful Lord, and never to be ashamed to worship openly with all their hearts.

LOVE YOUR SPOUSE ABOVE YOUR CHILDREN

In terms of inspiring a child to adore God, this principle is probably the most important. Its negative rendering is even more piercing: If you want to ensure that your child will always have difficulty worshiping God, then fail to love your spouse openly. This can affect your child adversely for life. Note that I am not referring to obvious evil like physical or verbal abuse. Merely the *absence of overt affection* between parents can raise doubts within a child that can later transfer to misgivings, insecurity and distrust.

We have already seen how parents should not argue in front of children but should take their disagreements to the privacy of their room. Now we go a step further: showing open affection. This, of course, does *not* mean sexual embraces; it does include hugs and kisses appropriate for public viewing. Each couple will have its own unique ways to express affection. As children routinely see great love expressed between their parents, they are filled with confidence that the household is in good order, that all is well at the top.

To this day, I remember with warmth a daily occurrence in my home as a child. When Dad came home from work, Mom dropped everything (including playing with me!) and hurried to the door to greet him. They had a long, lingering kiss and hug as we children watched. It was clear to us that they did not want the embrace to stop, but Dad finally turned to greet us children heartily. While some of my classmates worried about all the arguments their parents were having, I knew that my household was stable. Such overt affection was a constant reminder of this security.

Furthermore, I knew that Dad's first priority was Mom (not me), and that Mom's first priority was Dad (not me). Rather than feel insulted or ignored, I knew instinctively that this was

God's order for the home. When a parent shows more love for a child than for a spouse, this actually increases the child's insecurity and self-centeredness. The best way to raise a worshiping child is to love your spouse as Christ loves the Church, putting the spouse first and then the child—without anything in between: job, career, hobbies. Obviously, this is not applicable to single parents, to whom the Lord gives particular grace.

Incidentally, in giving this advice, it is taken for granted that every parent's first love is truly the Lord. Nothing should ever come between you and God, not your church, not your children, not even your spouse. "Love the Lord your God with all your heart and with all your soul and with all your mind and with all your strength" (Mark 12:30). Not only is this our first priority as Christians, but living this priority before our children is our first priority as parents.

Therefore, the correct order is God, your spouse, your child and then everything else. When children sense that their parents' world is in the right order, then it is easier for them to get their world together. It creates a long-term stability that will establish God as the center of their world, which indeed He is! It provides them with the warmth and security portrayed in Robert Browning's famous poem that concludes:

> God's in his heaven:
> All's right with the world.

8

Your Church's Youth Ministry

> *It was he who gave some to be apostles,*
> *some to be prophets, some to be evange-*
> *lists, and some to be pastors and teachers,*
> *to prepare God's people for works of*
> *service, so that the body of Christ may*
> *be built up.*
>
> EPHESIANS 4:11–12

et us take a closer look at the areas of your church that minister specifically to your children and thus have a considerable impact on their worship experience. Of course, every church is unique, and the size of your church has a great deal to do with its youth ministry (or lack thereof). You may belong to a mega-church with a huge staff or a small congregation with volunteers.

Whatever the size or denomination of your church, the purpose of the youth ministry should remain the same. Its object, its *raison d'être,* is to assist parents in raising their children to follow Christ. How this is done may take a million different forms, from soccer games to Bible studies. But its effectiveness is measured, not in numbers of activities, but in how well this object is achieved. Dietrich Bonhoeffer remarked: "The test of the morality of a society is what it does for its children." Whether it be a society, a civilization or a local church, this standard remains paramount.

In the twenty or so years that your children will attend your church, they will generally pass through three stages of youth ministry: (1) nursery, (2) Sunday school classes and (3) teenage youth groups. Other groups that may follow, like college groups, will be considered as extensions of our third stage. The first two stages take place on Sunday morning. The third may occur at other places and at different times of the week.

Before examining these three stages of youth ministry, let us first consider the relationship between youth ministries and parents.

YOUTH EVANGELISM OR YOUTH DISCIPLESHIP OR BOTH?

The Great Commission Jesus gave us, to "go and make disciples of all nations" (Matthew 28:19), is a two-part command. The first part is evangelism, proclaiming the Gospel in order to bring people to Christ. The second is training these new Christians, encouraging their fruitfulness and spiritual maturity, a process called discipleship.

These are two distinct actions. And as with many comple-
mentary tasks, trying to do both simultaneously incurs the risk
of accomplishing neither. An orchestra conductor needs both
of his arms to conduct, for they have different functions. His
right arm principally establishes and maintains correct tempo
and meter, while his left expresses dynamics, phrasing and
subtle nuances. If he tries to do both functions simultaneously with one arm he will convey nothing but confusion to
the orchestra.

In the same way, the Church is called to evangelism and to
discipleship. Yet we sometimes try to do both functions at once,
resulting in confused believers as well as confused unbelievers. If
a preacher gives a "salvation message" each Sunday, for instance,
the believers in the congregation will not be taught the many
other truths of the Bible. This is why some churches opt for
two different services, a "seeker" service as well as a "regular"
service for believers.

How does this dual concept work in youth ministry? The
typical approach is often a jumbled mix of evangelism and
discipleship. Some large churches actually have a youth pastor
and a youth evangelist. The former takes care of the young
Christians, while the latter tries to bring the Gospel to young
unbelievers. But most churches do not have such a prodigious
staff available, and youth workers are often called to wear
many hats.

Nevertheless, the principles given in this chapter are based
on the fundamental tenet that the primary purpose of youth
ministry in your church is *to serve the children of the church's adult members,* who, presumably, are believers. This is not to belittle those
outstanding workers whose vision is to introduce unbelieving
youth to Christ. It is simply to bring youth ministry into the
scope of this book, which is written to believing parents who
desire to teach their children a lifestyle of worship.

YOUTH MINISTRIES ASSIST, NOT REPLACE, PARENTS

One of the many ramifications of confusing evangelism and discipleship happens frequently at Christian schools. Years ago I taught at an institution that enrolled children from believing families as well as those from unbelievers. This excellent school had high standards and was often quite successful in bringing whole families to the Lord. Yet its policy of accepting students who were not believers sometimes led to awkward situations, one of which illustrates my next point.

One student was particularly rebellious and constantly in trouble. His parents went to church but (by their own admission) failed to take the Bible's teaching very seriously. At a Christian school conference they made this remarkable statement to me: "We can't do anything with him! That's why we brought him here. We're paying you to fix him for us!"

Well, we tried. But it was no surprise that our efforts were not successful. It was never in God's plan that youth ministries or Christian schools should do the actual work of parenting. They are to *assist* Christian parents, not replace them.

This is, of course, important for those in youth ministry to realize. Any youth worker who ignores his or her parents (even bad parents) and attempts to usurp their position is in the wrong job. Granted, becoming a surrogate parent is always a temptation. Most youth workers know the children well, but not their parents. Furthermore, they often work with children whose parents are not fulfilling their spiritual duties. Nevertheless, *they are the parents* God has given these children.

It is even more important for Christian parents to realize the true position of youth workers: They are neither substitute parents nor babysitters. In other words, Christian parents must never find themselves saying what the couple said to me at the conference. No, the parents must prayerfully "fix the children themselves" and never thrust their parental roles upon others.

THE PARENT'S ROLE IN YOUTH MINISTRIES

So what is the best role that you as a parent can play in the youth ministry of the church? Certainly, you should pray for the youth ministry, its leaders and young people, but you are not a full-time church worker and are probably not trained to serve as one. Furthermore, the church staff spends much of every week planning youth ministry activities, and you, of course, do not have much input in its decisions.

The best role a parent can (and should) play in the church's youth ministries is twofold—and these two roles are intricately linked. The first is that of a *faithful volunteer* and the second is that of *submissive counsel.* Consider the importance of each role.

Any church staff member knows that the real work of the church is done by volunteers. The pastor and staff cannot do everything! Indeed, their role is "to prepare God's people for works of service" (Ephesians 4:12). There should be no spectators in the Church; each of us needs to find his place, to be directly involved. The Body of Christ, including each local church, "grows and builds itself up in love, as each part does its work" (Ephesians 4:16).

If you have children in any of the youth ministries at your church, then this should be the first place to volunteer. Every nursery, Sunday school program and youth group needs parents to take a part. This may be difficult for some, especially mothers of large families, who, after a week of chasing kids, would be happy to dump them off with the church workers and take a break. When I see rambunctious toddlers and their exhausted mothers, I remember a quote of Ralph Waldo Emerson: "There never was a child so lovely, but his mother was glad to get him asleep." Nevertheless, we know that abandoning our children to a nursery without becoming involved is really not a healthy option if we truly want the best for them.

The second role, that of counselor to your church's youth workers, is predicated somewhat on the first role of volunteering. You may have information about specific needs of your children, for instance, or you may have information to share about an area of spiritual progress in their lives. A youth worker will be far more willing to hear and accept your counsel if you have long been known for your faithful volunteering. This is no place to drop off your children and then try to tell the staff how to do its job. Instead, be the parent always willing to help. Show a submissive spirit. Then when the time comes to share your feelings, they will be readily accepted. Remember, parents must respect the authority of each church worker. The pastor is their boss; you are not.

WHEN YOU SEE ROOM FOR CHANGE

We need to consider this topic on a higher level. Suppose you go to a fine church with strong biblical teaching, but one that does not happen to have much emphasis on youth ministry. Should you try to change this situation? In fact, *can* you change this situation?

Much of my adult life has been spent working for the local church, including hundreds (thousands?) of meetings to discuss church programs. I can assure you that all those great ideas do not come from the pastor or even the staff—they are suggested by faithful members of the church. In fact, looking back over the years it seems to me that *all* the best and most successful ideas came, not from the church leadership, but from the congregation.

But I must not fail to mention: The wonderful suggestions came from *dedicated* church members, ones who were then ready to roll up their sleeves and work. We also received a myriad of comments from people who simply wanted to dump their suggestions on us and leave, giving us more work to do! As you might imagine, this second type of suggestion giver was not very welcome.

In other words, if God shows you a deficiency in your church's youth program, He does not want you to leave the problem with the church leadership. He showed you the problem because He wants you to help with its solution. Before you mention the matter to anyone else, pray! Seek the Lord for ideas in which you could be a prime mover, not a complainer. If you find that you have only negative comments about the youth program, consider the words of Scripture: "Don't grumble against each other, brothers, or you will be judged. The Judge is standing at the door!" (James 5:9).

If you believe that God wants you to bring something to the attention of the church leadership, call and make an appointment—with the right person. Begin with the person who is specifically in charge of youth ministry, avoiding the temptation to go over his or her head and directly to the pastor. Remember to make your approach in humility. You are there to help, not grumble.

Never forget: The openness to your ideas will usually be in proportion to the amount of faithful service you have already rendered the church. This is as it should be.

YOUTH MINISTRY: THE CHURCH NURSERY

With all of this in mind, we come to the first stage of your church's youth ministry: the nursery. Remember that we are looking at this from the parent's point of view, not, for instance, as if we were designing the perfect church nursery program. This is not the parents' job. As we have seen above, our position as parents is to help out by our volunteering and our counsel.

Before you leave your infant or toddler at the nursery for the first time, check it out. The two primary ingredients of a nursery are *personnel* and *facility*. The former is the most important, since you are entrusting your children into their hands. Do they seem competent, caring, positive? Are they old enough—many nurseries use young workers—to take charge in an emergency? (I remember when a young worker let one of our babies roll off the changing table!) Are other parents involved or is everyone hired by the church?

These and other questions will occur to you, as you assess the nursery's personnel. Remember that your child's *earliest impressions of going to church* will be affected by these people, and you want these memories to be good ones. Talk to the nursery's director, not only to volunteers, to find all you can about the program. In these times, you must even check to make certain that none of the workers has any record of child molestation. Whoever the individual workers may be, keep in mind that the nursery program will usually reflect the characteristics of its leadership. The more you can get to know and help the nursery program's director, the better.

As to the actual facility, the three items to look for are cleanliness, separation of different ages and ability to contact you quickly. The cleanliness issue is obvious, and far more significant than whether or not your church happens to own the latest newfangled nursery equipment. Separation of ages is important, especially keeping loud toddlers away from sleeping babies. And the nursery should have a reliable system of contacting parents, either electronically or in person. Which means you have a responsibility to inform the workers where you are in the church itself.

Ultimately, the best way to improve your church's nursery is to take part. When the first Sunday comes for your little one to experience the nursery, it might be good for you to volunteer. This helps the child become acclimated to the new situation. But long after your children are accustomed to the nursery environment, you need to be involved—not only for your own children but to support the entire program.

YOUTH MINISTRY: SUNDAY SCHOOL CLASSES

Most churches encourage school-age children to attend Sunday school classes, presumably with their own age groups. Depending upon the size of the church, the number of workers available and the facility limitations, these might include a kindergarten class, a first grade class, etc. In some situations, this may include a large multi-age meeting often called Children's Church.

Whatever the particulars about your church's meetings for youth, you want them to make a significant impact on your children. Again, the best way to help is to volunteer your services. Many people who had never thought of themselves as teachers found that when they gave it a try, this gift was within them. There are literally thousands of testimonies to the powerful difference one Sunday school teacher made in the life of a child.

You will likely be given a curriculum to follow, but remember above all to *make it fun for the students*. Rather than reading a long passage from the Word, have the students act it out. Rather than asking a list of questions about the Bible, divide the class into teams and play "Bible Baseball." The difference between a mediocre Sunday school teacher and a great one is not always the actual content of teaching, but the manner in which it was presented.

Even if teaching itself is not a possibility, no class would turn down a willing helper. Having a helping hand can make an otherwise shy student become involved in the classroom activities. Sunday school classes often have children visiting who may not know anyone and need extra attention. Talk to the Sunday school director to find what other needs you may be able to fill.

As you look over a classroom full of students, consider the amazing potential of each child. Billy Graham was just another kid in such a classroom; so were thousands of other outstanding people. You never know how far a smile or a kind word may go. This is why Scripture impels us to "be kind and compassionate to one another" (Ephesians 4:32). Sometimes even the smallest gesture of love can be a turning point in a life.

Do not assume that every child in a Sunday school class comes from a strong family, with the loving support of two Christian parents. Sadly, this is less likely every year. Many of the students may have only one parent, who is exhausted and overwhelmed with keeping the family together. Others may be lonely, neglected or abused. For some children, the only time of their week when the love of God is felt is in a Sunday class. Consider the profound words of Frederick Douglass: "It is easier to build strong children than to repair broken men." Teaching in your church's Sunday school is a golden opportunity to let your light shine for Christ.

Concerning your own children's classes, it is essential to be involved. If you are not physically present, then always ask about the class afterward. Rather than saying, "Did you have a nice time?" ask for details. Show them that you are interested and that you consider the Sunday school class important. A few extra moments each week will pay high dividends over the many years of child rearing.

Youth Ministry: Youth Group

A youth group for teenagers may be the most important ministry within a local church. Children in junior high and senior high school go through so many physical and emotional changes, and have so many negative influences all around them, that they desperately need a safe place with true friends in order to grow spiritually. Furthermore, teens critically need biblical teaching about dating, relationships and purity. Having friends with biblical standards will definitely help your child accept your standards. The difference between having a good youth group and not having one can easily become the difference between a teenager following Christ and one falling away from the faith.

Youth groups, of course, meet at different times. Whatever the time or location, get your teens there. Our youth group meets at a house 28 miles away from us, but, with four teenage sons, we have made certain they rarely miss a meeting. I think we would rather miss Sunday morning church! If your teens can drive, give them the keys and pay for the gasoline. It may be the best investment you will ever make.

A typical youth meeting will consist of worship music (you may not like it, but they will!), fellowship, perhaps some games and a short teaching. The content is important, but so is the concept of *belonging*. Learning to worship the Lord without mom and dad around is indispensable and will further their spiritual maturity more than the best of Sunday morning experiences.

This is a controversial point, but I believe that it is important for Christian teens to gather together (in *groups*) with believers of the opposite sex. Your church's youth group should create a safe environment for boys and girls to promote godly, pure relationships. Many Christian marriages actually began with two young people getting to know each other at such meetings.

135

This is a far better environment than the many alternatives the world offers today.

Since dynamic leadership is essential to youth ministry, the parent needs to do everything possible to support the youth group's leader. Your own teens should know that you have a good relationship with the leader. Let me put it this way: If you are able to invite either the pastor or the youth leader to dinner, invite the youth leader.

What is the best way for you to help with your church's youth group? Remember the two-fold role of volunteering and counsel. The leader will listen to the counsel of a parent who has driven carloads of teenagers to various activities. If you are concerned about some teaching he has given, do not rebuke him in front of others. Ask for a private meeting to discuss your concern. Your counsel, given in the right spirit, can greatly help the direction of the youth group, enabling it to minister to your children—and many others as well.

YOUR INFLUENCE ON OTHER YOUNG CHRISTIANS

Let us take a step back from your influence within your church, and consider how the Lord might use you as a blessing to the peers of your children. Of course, your first concern should be the spiritual benefit of your own children. Yet as they see you in such ministry, and recognize the respect their friends give you, your children will be quicker to respond to your leadership.

Today's teens are desperately looking for role models. As writer Carolyn Coats puts it, "Children have more need of models than of critics." Many kids come from dysfunctional homes and cannot find the spiritual leadership they need. If they look at their church and still cannot find credible role models, then where will they go? I am afraid that the world will be happy to oblige.

Parents must realize that every time they go to church, they are examples before the eyes of many young people. They may be examples of understanding and encouragement. Or they may be—usually without knowing it—examples of people who have no time for others, who are troubled with their own problems and cannot be bothered with teenagers. In short, examples of hypocrisy. If teens in your church perceive this, they will find more accepting examples elsewhere.

This Sunday notice the young people in your congregation. You may or may not know them by name. Ask the Lord to give you a burden for the hurting youth who are all around us. When you see a group of young people, recall Jesus' words to His disciples: "I tell you, open your eyes and look at the fields! They are ripe for harvest" (John 4:35). Ask God how you can help bring encouragement to a teenager who thinks that no one cares. One act or word of kindness may keep a wavering youth in the fold and give her the reassurance she needs to follow Christ.

Talk to your children about their friends; show sincere concern. You may be able to give good advice to help them minister to those around them. And as you show compassion to the friends they love, a new bond of fellowship will grow between you.

ENCOURAGING YOUR CHILDREN INTO MINISTRY

The previous paragraph brings us to our next point. In the same way that we parents are admonished to be participants—not spectators—in our church, so our children should be similarly admonished. In fact, the children who bring their faith into adulthood are generally those who were heavily involved in different types of ministry for years beforehand. The principle is simple: It is much easier for a private to slip away from the Army than for a general to do so.

In what ways should you encourage your children in ministry? This, of course, depends upon the various talents and temperaments of the children themselves. Some are natural-born leaders and can take charge of a youth meeting. Others are more servant-oriented and would rather work in a "behind-the scenes" capacity. Still others might be relational and able to counsel their peers. Paul aptly compares the different gifts within the Church as various parts of the body, and adds, "But in fact God has arranged the parts in the body, every one of them, just as he wanted them to be" (1 Corinthians 12:18).

It is the parent's job to discern these talents and temperaments within children and to help match them with the appropriate ministries. For example, your daughter may have a lovely singing voice, but if the church has no real need for a soloist, then something else needs to be explored. It takes time, but it is always worth the effort. Helping your children find their places within the church is one of the great joys of parenting, and one that is all too frequently neglected in the hassle of keeping a household running. As American writer Marcelene Cox reminds us, "Parents are often so busy with the physical rearing of children, that they miss the glory of parenthood, just as the grandeur of trees is lost when raking leaves."

Whatever situation you consider, keep in mind the importance of your child's being *successful*. If you put children in a no-win situation, the failure may discourage future ministry possibilities, actually pushing them away from the church. We want them to succeed in their assays into ministry so that they will desire to go further and further.

Let us consider a few possibilities. Can your children help in the church nursery? Can they sing in the choir? How about join-

ing the visitation to elderly church members? What about helping to set up (and clean up) for church events? Most churches
have such a long list of jobs that they would love to have more
volunteers—of any age.

A great place to encourage your children to help is within
the youth ministry itself. Many Sunday school programs need
young helpers. Often a teenage youth group will form a leadership committee to plan events, and in this way your children can
have a direct influence on the ministry of the group. These are
excellent opportunities for your children, even if it means you
have a new place to drive them each week.

Yet another possibility for your teens is to be counselors
at church camps and vacation Bible school. Such interaction
between them and younger children is true ministry indeed!
Suddenly your children become role models, and as they recognize this fact, their own behavior is affected positively. This
experience also prepares them for future jobs by helping them
develop important people skills.

Finally, a word must be said about mission trips. Many excellent ministries and large churches offer short-term mission trips
for teenagers. These can be eye-opening, life-changing experiences. Whether it be housing repairs in a poverty-stricken area
or evangelistic outreach at the beach, such ministry makes a
powerful impression. I have known young people who were
barely interested in spiritual matters come back from a short
mission trip on fire for the Lord. Soon you will find them praying to "the Lord of the harvest . . . to send out workers into his
harvest field" (Luke 10:2).

If you want your children to be worshipers for life, then the
earlier they become directly involved with their church the
better.

9

Corporate Worship and Children

It is good to praise the LORD and make
music to your name, O Most High.

PSALM 92:1

We have seen that worship is a great deal more than singing. Worship is the adoration of God that encompasses all of life, whether we praise Him in our cars or meditate on Scripture while in line at the bank. It does not take a church building, a congregation or a choir. It takes only a heart that longs to worship the Lord.

Having said this, we also recognize that corporate worship, coming together as a body to offer our praises, is vital to the

Christian life. It is encouraged in many biblical passages: "Praise God in the great congregation" (Psalm 68:26). And one of our regular opportunities for corporate worship takes place at church every Sunday. Christian parents naturally want their children to worship the Lord corporately as well as in their private devotions.

"Aye, there's the rub," as Hamlet would say. Many children do not like to open their mouths during Sunday worship. Teenage boys are probably the main offenders in this area, but the problem infects thousands of Christian children who, for one reason or another, do not wholeheartedly participate in corporate worship. This chapter will examine why this is so as well as offer some practical solutions. We will begin at your church, but the journey will take us through your house, to your children's friends and deep inside the children themselves—to the fears and insecurities that can hinder worship.

A CHILD'S VIEW OF CHURCH

Let us start with the fundamentals: We want our children to *like* going to church. We want them to enjoy the experience and to have a growing love for worshiping the Lord. We want them to look forward to Sunday morning, to be glad that they are Christians. We hope that they will pray as the poet George Herbert prayed: "Thou who has given so much to me, give me one thing more: a grateful heart."

We must never forget this point. This is our object, the goal we are shooting for, and we must keep it in mind. Because, as if you didn't know, going to church with children can be quite a hassle! We need to remind ourselves constantly *why* we are doing all this and to stay focused on our fundamental goal.

As we have seen, our children's earliest views of church will imitate their parents' views of church. This is a good thing to remember on Sunday morning—when the kids are arguing, the breakfast is burnt and the tire is flat. If we convey to them that going to church is a huge bother, we are planting the wrong seeds. Instead, they need to see their parents' pleasure in participating at church, that their parents truly love to worship God with the saints.

This overall attitude of "looking forward to church" needs to start at the earliest possible age. If your baby is afraid of the church nursery's babysitters, for instance, he may develop an association between going to church and something quite unpleasant. Take time to talk with the nursery workers and other parents to help your child adjust.

Or suppose your children engage in the "squirminess" factor: Parents want their little ones to sit quietly through church, but the youngsters have no such desire. If the parents are harsh enough, they might (I doubt it) succeed in keeping them quiet, but this short-term outcome could have a high long-term price. The children learn to dread church, especially if "that's where my parents are meanest."

There are alternatives to harshness. When our children were young, we bought special four-color pens, which delighted them. Our rule was that these could only be used on Sunday morning. So from an early age, they could not wait to get to church each week. They knew that when we arrived and were seated, Dad would give them a notebook and a marvelous four-color pen with which to draw quietly during the service. They looked forward to this from Monday to Saturday.

Remember that you, the parent, have possibly been going to church for many years, yet this is a much newer experience for your children. When one tries something new, one generally starts slowly with a small taste and continues if that taste is pleasant. Our position as parents is to encourage the children to "taste and see that the LORD is good" (Psalm 34:8).

143

MEETING WITH CHURCH FRIENDS

An essential factor in helping your children enjoy going to church concerns friends. This cannot be emphasized enough. If children have good friends at their church, then they look forward to Sunday morning. If they do not have good friends at church, then they do not look forward to Sunday morning. It is that simple.

Very few children actually enjoy going to a church where they do not know anyone. We adults have matured and learned the social skills that make talking to strangers a simple matter, but we should not assume that this is so for our children. They may be quite insecure in this area, and the thought of attending a Sunday school class with a room full of strangers may render them too sick to stand.

Family vacations bring this to light. My wife and I would be happy to visit a church wherever we might be, but our children would rather have a "family church" service. It is not so much that our children are shy (far from it!). Rather, it shows how important it is to them to have fellowship with Christian friends of their own ages. Friends are a supremely significant part of our children's Christian experience.

This can be a particular problem if you attend a small church. The parents may find all the fellowship they need, but there may not be many children the same ages as your own. Then you have trouble. Children will usually become bored and often miserable. Enough years of such wretchedness—the child associating loneliness and misery with the church as well as God Himself—and this child may have a difficult time worshiping the Lord.

It is no good to tell a child: "You should just focus on God; we don't go to church to meet our friends." Such an argument assumes a high level of spiritual maturity. There are few children who, if given a choice to spend time with their friends or spend time with God, would choose the latter. Forcing this upon young children will only cause them to resent the church and the Lord.

For many parents in this situation, I am afraid the answer is difficult: It generally involves a change of churches. If such a radical move seems shocking to you, refer to chapter 4. At the end of that chapter we saw that it is more important for the children to enjoy church than it is for the parents. Once your children are out of toddling and diapers, they truly need friends at church. This not only provides needed fellowship in the short term, but it undergirds a positive perception of going to a place of corporate worship.

In fact, the more you can do to make Sunday a special day, the better. We always see that homework is finished on Saturday so that Sunday afternoons and evenings are free for family and friends. Sometimes we have an ad hoc family time or a short trip. Sometimes our children's friends come over to our house after church. God gave us the Sabbath not only for our rest but to keep our church and the experience of corporate worship in the center of our lifestyles.

IS SUNDAY MORNING AN *ADULT* EXPERIENCE AT YOUR CHURCH?

Doubtless some readers of this book are pastors or church leaders, but most of us are faithful congregants with little input as to the structure and emphasis of our Sunday morning worship services. We need to be careful, therefore, as we examine the service itself and avoid the devilish temptation to become critical. The Scriptures make our duty to the church leadership clear: "Obey them so that their work will be a joy, not a burden, for that would be of no advantage to you" (Hebrews 13:17).

We are considering the Sunday service in order to gauge its effect on your children. We are not here to be critics; the Lord does not need one and neither does your pastor. He or she must be sensitive to God's leading in order to minister to the whole church, not just your family. If he tries to please you, he will not please someone else. His job is to try to please the Lord.

With this in mind, consider a typical Sunday morning at your church. Every church is unique, but most services include several elements: prayer, Scripture reading, a sermon and a time of corporate worship (usually represented by singing Christian songs). Presumably the prayer, Scripture reading and sermon are geared to the adults of the church, though the older children are (we hope) also edified. Perhaps the younger ones are in Sunday school classes or Children's Church during that time.

Now, what about the worshipful singing? Is it primarily an adult experience? Should it be? What about the children? Should they be expected to sing the adult songs with gusto? Or should there be children's songs? And are the adults to sing them with gusto?

What to do?

THE IMPOSSIBILITY OF PLEASING EVERYONE WITH MUSIC

Having been a minister of music at various churches for my entire adult life, I have come to realize the truth of the old adage: "You can't please everyone all of the time." In other words, there are *no* songs that everyone likes, not even your favorites! You may not believe it, but if you name your favorite worship song, I can assure you that there are people (probably in your church) who cannot stand it. And there are songs that you cannot stand that are deeply loved by others.

Once when speaking to a church about music, I mentioned an old song that had actually been voted by a national poll as one of the worst songs ever written. In an attempt not to be sued, I will call this song "Bug." When I read some of the ridiculous lyrics of this song to the congregation, we howled with laughter. Yet after the sermon, a member of the church came up to me and said, "I love the song 'Bug.' If I had had a tomato with me this morning, I would have used it on you!" She was not smiling.

People have strong feelings about the music they like and even stronger feelings about the music they do not like. This state of affairs led composer Richard Wagner to complain: "The immoral profession of music criticism must be abolished!" Unfortunately, it has not been. It is within each one of us. Furthermore, there is a generational element present. Senior citizens generally do not like the songs of teenagers, and children generally do not like the songs of their parents. They may tolerate them, of course, but they will never embrace them as their own.

Indeed, each generation has always attempted to find or create certain styles that are uniquely its own. Today, there is often a battle between those who enjoy the old hymns and those who like a more contemporary sound—but this is not a new situation. When Isaac Watts (1674–1748) brought out his hymns, those who were used to the old chorales rejected this "new style." Later, when Isaac Watts' hymns were the norm, the Wesleys' hymns were considered too modern. Still later, when the Wesleyan hymns were standard, revivalist Fanny Crosby's hymns became the newfangled music. And so it goes throughout history.

With this in mind, you can see that there are no worship songs that will satisfy everyone in your congregation. Therefore, even if you harangued your minister of music (I do not recommend this!) into presenting only songs that your children like to sing, it would not work. The rest of the church would revolt against your choices.

147

THE VARIETY OF MUSIC

Earlier I said that people have strong feelings about the music they like and dislike. Perhaps stronger than they need to be. A bit of *deference* toward the favorite music of others could do all of us a great deal of good. There are hundreds of different styles of music today. Liking or disliking them should really not matter so much to us.

I have studied music intensely for more than thirty years, received a doctorate in music, conducted many orchestras, written several books about music, taught at the college level and lectured about a variety of musical topics. Yet the more I know about music, the more I realize that I do *not* know. There is so much more to be discovered that I have barely scratched the surface. It is difficult, I must admit, not to be amused by the many people (all musical laymen) who consider themselves experts. Of course, they are really only experts *in what they happen to like and dislike.*

Each of us needs to take his opinions less seriously, especially his musical opinions. Furthermore, we need to extend this teaching to our children so that we might be able to worship God with a wide variety of music. It can be done, and it should be done. Scripture commands, "Honor one another above yourselves" (Romans 12:10), and this goes for our musical opinions, too. Those songs you do not like are really not so bad. And those songs you love are probably not so great either! (The same could be said about your teenager's music.)

The best advice I have ever read about comparing the merits of different styles of music was written by a non-musician: C. S. Lewis. He ended an article about church music with this profound sentence: "For all our offerings, whether of music or martyrdom, are like the intrinsically worthless present of a child, which a father values indeed, but values only for the intention."

In other words, it matters little if you like traditional hymns or the latest in contemporary music. The important thing is the state of your heart.

DEVELOPING OUR MUSICAL TASTES

The most important thing that we can teach our children about music—especially worship music—is to *appreciate its variety.* We must learn to set aside our opinions and focus on worshiping the Lord. On a given Sunday morning it does not matter if we sing Christian rock or "Rock of Ages." Nor does it matter if it involves a pipe organ or synthesized drums. Nor does it matter if the song is too fast or too slow or pitched too high or too low. What matters is whether or not our hearts are focused on Jesus Christ.

Traveling to different churches, I often find parents or grandparents who are worried because the young people in their church "don't know the old hymns anymore." I, too, have a great love for hymnology and certainly do not think we should throw away this rich musical heritage. Nevertheless, I ask these concerned souls, "Since you want the young people to learn about the music you like, are you willing to learn about the music *they* like?" As you may imagine, this produces some worried looks.

Such stretching of our musical tastes is not easy for any of us. My wife and I are both professional classical musicians, so our entire lives have been surrounded by Bach, Beethoven and the rest of the great masters. Imagine our faces when our oldest son began playing loud contemporary Christian music from his room. Our first reaction was to call the police! All we could think was "Where did we go wrong?!"

I am glad to say that God gave us grace to calm down and pray. Instead of letting music create a serious barrier in our relationship—all too common in families today—we began to listen to our son's music with him. Soon we had to admit that some of it (not all) was quite well done. This led to meaningful discussions (not quarrels) about *what is excellent,* which Paul admonishes us to keep in mind (see Philippians 4:8). Rather than argue about the merits of different styles of music, our conversations tended toward ways of identifying *the best* endeavors from within each style.

Such conversations should take place in every Christian family and begin when the children are still quite small. Whenever possible, expose your children to a variety of musical styles, always trying to find the best in each.

Not only will exposing your young children to different types of music save you from needless arguments with your teenagers, it will also enable them to worship the Lord in a variety of different musical settings: old hymns, folk music, classical music and, yes, rock music. When your teenager's friends are rolling their eyes at a dusty hymn, your child may be singing from the heart. And when an upbeat number is played and many parents are huffing with disapproval, your family will be worshiping God together.

INSECURITY ABOUT SINGING

Thus we see that musical tastes can hinder your children from entering into Sunday morning worship. But let us suppose that they are open to many different styles of music. Is the problem of engaging them in worship solved? No. We face another important factor: It takes a good deal of inner security and confidence to sing in *any* public setting.

By this, I am not referring to soprano solos at Carnegie Hall. Even when hidden in a large congregation, many children (and adults!) are intimidated and self-conscious about opening their mouths in song: *What if someone nearby actually hears me! What if I make a mistake and suddenly sing something all by myself!*

The fear of "sticking out" strikes most of us at some level; it is almost omnipresent in adolescents. For teenage boys in particular the fear of singing in public can be excruciating, and its insecurities continue into the lives of the bravest men. I know a highly decorated war veteran who would rather be back in combat than have to sing at church. It amazes me that having bullets and grenades zing over one's head does not produce such terror as the possibility of being heard by one's fellow worshiper.

If you, the parent, happen to struggle with such fears, you will not like this paragraph. We must again consider your duty of *modeling* those things that you want your children to emulate. We simply cannot expect our children to do what we refuse to do. Therefore, we, as parents, need to take the initiative by singing out in their presence (at church and home), whether we happen to feel good about our singing or not.

The best solution to this problem is to start while your children are still young. Let them enjoy singing before the inhibitions of adolescence are upon them. Then keep them singing year after year. I like to quote Elizabethan composer William Byrd: "Since singing is so good a thing, I wish all men would learn to sing." Sing with them at every opportunity. Say, "You've got a nice voice." (Probably it is even true.)

Sing together wherever you can: at home, in the car, during family devotionals. Encourage them to sing *anything:* Christmas carols, Americana folk tunes, Beatles' songs, whatever they like. If your church has a youth choir or your region has a community chorus, see if they have an opening. The more singing of any kind your children do, the more they will be free to sing unto the Lord in worship.

Surely, one of the most important duties of a parent is to do everything we can to build our children's confidence. John tells us that "perfect love drives out fear" (1 John 4:18) and our unconditional acceptance will give our children boldness and security. This will make a huge difference throughout their lives and enable them to worship the Lord in many different settings without fear.

Music Lessons, Anyone?

This section may surprise some of you, who might be asking, "What do music lessons have to do with teaching our children to worship?" They have everything to do with it. Another reason that many people—even typically confident people—do not join in worship at church is because they feel that they do not know anything about music. They hear others around them singing harmony with ease, and they perceive themselves as inexperienced and intimidated.

Can this be prevented? Quite easily. For many people music is a mysterious, incomprehensible topic. But it does not have to be so. In fact, just a few music lessons with a qualified teacher can open one's eyes and ears to a whole new world—a world in which one can join in without fear.

To begin with, Christian parents should consider private music lessons for their children. "Why *private* lessons?" you ask. "Why not have Billy learn tuba in a classroom the way he learned algebra and grammar? Can't music be learned in a group setting?" Yes, much of it can. Many schools offer excellent classroom courses taught by inspiring music educators with wonderful results. These are usually "general music" type classes (or chorus, band and orchestra rehearsals), but it is certainly possible to teach the basics of individual instruments like the tuba in a group setting.

Nevertheless, the best way to learn music is one on one. If your children are particularly talented, it would be unthinkable for them to have only classroom instruction and never have private lessons. In fact, classroom instruction alone can be detrimental to their ongoing musical progress. Even if they have not shown extraordinary talent, the experience will be a great boost to their desire to worship. As to which instrument, consider both your child's desires as well as the practicality of finding an instrument and an excellent teacher. You might also consider vocal lessons.

Indeed, the study of music results in many non-musical benefits. In one of my earlier books, I discussed seventeen extra benefits that are achieved through learning music. They are

Perseverance
Confidence
Responsibility
Discipline
Identity and self-esteem
Love of music, art, culture and history
Precision and motor control
Identification of talents
Teamwork
Using time wisely
Following directions
Overcoming nervousness
Increasing intelligence
Commitment to excellence
Finding like-minded peers
Creativity and self-expression
Spiritual nurturing

It all boils down to this: You want your children to be comfortable and assured in their adoration of God. Much of this involves singing in a group setting. One of the best ways to be confident and uninhibited in such singing situations is to develop a background in music. A weekly music lesson, therefore, can be a great tool for encouraging your child to a life of worship. It will take time, effort and money, of course, but the rewards far outweigh the costs. Our Lord's words inspire us to seek out training in music, as with all our pursuits, from an accomplished teacher: "A student is not above his teacher, but everyone who is fully trained will be like his teacher" (Luke 6:40).

THE BACKGROUND OF WORSHIP SONGS AND SONGWRITERS

Most of us feel a special closeness to a song if we know something about the reason it was written. Many songwriters preface their performance of a new song by telling the audience its background. This can be yet another inspiration for your children to sing to the Lord with all their hearts.

A hundred years ago, when virtually all Christians sang nineteenth-century hymns, the background of each song was found in books with titles like *Your Favorite Hymn Stories.* These books are still available today and contain many wonderful narratives. Probably each household should own one, so that in family devotional times you can give meaning to the singing of the old hymns. Hymnologist William J. Hart used to teach: "An effective method is to relate the story, then have the hymn sung . . . when thus used, the story and the hymn are linked together and thus form a lasting association."

But what about information on the newer songs that your children doubtless want to sing? This has been a problem for a number of years. True, biographies have been written about a few of the principal Christian songwriters, such as Bill Gaither, Keith Green and Michael Card. And the written material inside worship CDs sometimes gives background on the composition of each song.

Nevertheless, it was not until the growth of the Internet that we began to find materials on the majority of contemporary worship songs. Now we can type the title of a new song into a search engine and an amazing assortment of materials becomes available, often including interviews with the songwriters. Now the songs become *real* to your children.

Another excellent way to develop interest in compositions and composers is to take your children to concerts of Christian artists touring in your area. It is amazing how a song that you sing every week at your church can suddenly come alive when experienced in a different setting. Worship videos, which present corporate worship in a wide variety of musical styles, are now available at Christian bookstores and on the Internet.

Whatever tools you employ to encourage your children in corporate worship, one thing should never be forgotten. . . .

THE HEART OF WORSHIP

A few years ago Matt Redman wrote a lovely song that has inspired many worshipers and worship leaders. It is called "The Heart of Worship," and its message is both simple and profound. It asks God's forgiveness for the Hollywood-like techniques sometimes used by the "worship industry" and proclaims, "I'm going back to the heart of worship, where it's all about you, it's all about you, Jesus."

We want our children to be free to worship God in every setting, from huge corporate worship services to the intimacy of their private quiet times with the Lord. Thus, even though this chapter has discussed ways to help your child experience corporate worship, let me offer a word of caution. It is all too easy for your children to sing the Sunday songs with great gusto, with their hearts a thousand miles away.

In other words, the best way to teach your children to enter into corporate worship is to teach them how to *worship the Lord daily with all their hearts,* as David did: "I will extol the LORD at all times; his praise will always be on my lips" (Psalm 34:1). The greatest worshipers I have ever known come to church on Sunday ready to go; the pump is already primed because they have spent the week worshiping God. If we concentrate on teaching corporate worship, we may or may not succeed in our purpose. But if we concentrate on the encouragement of worshiping the Lord daily—in situations where it is purely between the child and God—we will succeed in creating a worshiper for all seasons.

10

The Different Stages
of Children's Worship

Train a child in the way he should go,
and when he is old he will not turn
from it.

PROVERBS 22:6

P oet John Wilmot (1647–1680) was a parent who grew in wisdom as his children grew in years. Late in his life, he wrote: "Before I got married, I had six theories about bringing up children. Now I

157

have six children and no theories." Most of us know exactly how he felt when he penned those words.

Ask any parent of a twenty year old and you will be told (correctly), "They grow up so fast!" Nevertheless, there are times of child rearing when you wonder if they will *ever* grow up! Indeed, in certain difficult times you cannot wait for them to finish that stage and move on to the next.

Yet they always do so. Children proceed from one stage to another, and certain aspects of parenting must change with them. When our sons were little, for instance, they were sometimes willfully rebellious and merited a spanking. Today, as they tower over our heads, we do not contemplate such an action. They still may deserve disciplinary action, but it involves more age-appropriate punishments—like the all-time favorite: withholding the car keys.

In the same way, as we raise our children to worship the Lord, we emphasize different actions at different times in their lives. This makes things a bit tricky if you have children in a variety of ages. But just as a toddler and a teenager eat different foods, so they will also need to be spiritually fed on an individual basis.

Many aspects of Christian child rearing, of course, must remain consistent year after year. Perhaps we had better explore this at greater length before we examine the specific stages of worship and child development.

WHAT SHOULD CHANGE
AND WHAT SHOULD NOT

Built to Last, an excellent book on business management by Jim Collins, studies a number of large corporations that have endured for many decades. In his careful analysis, Collins discovered two principles that each of these successful companies possessed. These points, in my own words, are: (1) Each company had a mission statement that was utterly unchangeable and would never be neglected, yet (2) the *manner* in which this mission was accomplished was completely flexible, changing freely from one idea to another.

We can see the parallel between Collins' fascinating findings and Christian parenting. Like those successful corporations, we parents need to have certain biblical principles that we hold onto without exception. But we also need to be flexible and creative as to their practical implementation. In other words, there are two categories of parenting concepts. The first is absolutely unchangeable and the second is absolutely flexible.

Jesus said that the Father commanded Him "what to say and how to say it" (John 12:49). When raising children, the basic "what to say" category remains constant. But "how you say it," that is, how these key principles are implemented, will change as your children move from infancy to young adulthood. The more clearly these two categories are understood the better.

We often see Christian parents going to war against each other because an item from the second category is mistakenly placed in the first. This is why, for instance, homeschool moms and non-homeschool moms are frequently at odds. You see, "providing our children a good education" is a first-category principle. But *how* that is to be done belongs in the second category with many possibilities and great flexibility. Even within the same family, different children may need different educational techniques and certain years may call for certain changes.

How do you determine what gets selected for the exalted first category? Every Christian couple needs to ask God's leading to answer this for their own family. Here are two points to help you as you pray. One, a first-category principle should be completely grounded in Scripture, not based on personal interpretation of an obscure verse. Two, your list of first-category principles should be *short,* containing only the highest priorities.

If you include too many items, it will be difficult to emphasize any of them.

Are there certain principles that should be included in the first category for every Christian family? Perhaps, but we must be cautious about determining the needs of other families. At most, I might venture to name three for each of us to consider: (1) love and respect for one another, (2) boundaries/responsibilities and, of course, (3) adoration of the Lord.

Whatever you place in your highest category, be flexible and creative in its implementation. This chapter will look at some of the different ways to inspire children of different ages to adore God. I hope that it will also serve as a model for the flexibility you will need to teach these and other topics you believe to be of prime importance.

WORSHIP TOOLS FOR YOUR USE

Now we move from our "unchangeable" first-category topic—*We desire to teach our children to worship*—to the "flexible" second-category implementation: *How will we teach them to worship?* In chapter 1 of this book, we considered the question What is worship? We discussed the definition: Worship is the private adoration of God. Then we examined some of the many different ways in which this private adoration can take place. Before we continue with age-specific direction, let us reexamine these worship tools, as some of them are more age appropriate for your children than others.

Some of the many ways in which we worship God include:

Singing at church
Reading the Bible
Singing alone

Meditating on Scripture
Speaking praise to God
Waiting on the Lord
Singing spontaneous (ad-lib) praise
Physical posturing (kneeling, dancing, etc.)
Praying in thanksgiving
Interceding
Studying the Bible
Celebrating Communion
Memorizing Scripture
Giving confession

These are all part of a Christian's "worship toolbox." Depending upon your background and denomination, you may have other items to add. Indeed, with the proper heart attitude, almost anything can be considered worship to the Lord: washing the dishes, mowing the grass, mopping the floor. Scripture teaches us, "Whatever you do, whether in word or deed, do it all in the name of the Lord Jesus, giving thanks to God the Father through him" (Colossians 3:17). This truly is a lifestyle of adoration.

Our toolbox should be as extensive as possible. Consider: Who will create a more vibrant painting, an artist with two colors on his palette or an artist with a dozen colors? Which chef will create the tastiest meal, one with three ingredients or one with twenty?

By the same token, suppose you hire a builder who owns a vast collection of tools. You think that you have made an excellent choice. But suppose this builder tries to turn screws with a hacksaw? Or hammer nails with a pipe wrench? You had better find a new builder! For one not only needs a good collection of tools but needs to know *when* and *how* to use each one correctly.

As parents we need a box full of worship tools, and we need to know the best time to use the right one.

A Worship Curriculum: Everything in Its Proper Order

Inspiring children to adore God means knowing when and how the various worship tools can be best used. You might not get very far insisting that junior high boys join you on visits to the local nursing home. But those same children might respond to gathering information on the computer for a Bible study. You probably will not get energetic five-year-old girls to sit and "wait on the Lord." But those youngsters will love singing and making hand motions to lively worship songs.

God, being a creative Lord, made us in such a way that we enjoy variety. Children in particular do not want to do the same things year after year, nor should they. A first grader does not study calculus and a teenager does not study the alphabet. Instead, the student moves year by year through a logical progression of studies that build upon themselves. As algebra prepares a student for geometry, so prayers of thanksgiving prepare your child for intercession. We need to fashion a worship curriculum in which the subjects complement each other and grow with every year.

One more point before we begin. Your child is different from everyone else's child. If you have more than one, then each one is different from the others. When David said, "O Lord, you have searched me and you know me" (Psalm 139:1), he affirmed that God recognizes each individual uniquely—and so should we as parents. A method that worked fine for one child may not work at all for another.

Watch that you do not try to fit your children into general, seemingly universal categories. Take, for instance, the label "the terrible twos." Our children were great when they were two; they went ballistic at around four.

Parents need to *know their children* in order to create a tailor-made model of worship. So as you consider the following worship curriculum, think about how it applies to your own children. Think creatively, making alterations as you deem best. We do not all have to have the same plan, but we do have to have *some* plan or our children may grow up before they learn to worship the Lord in ways that are truly meaningful to them.

Ages 1 to 6: The Years of Praise

From the lips of children and infants you have ordained praise.

PSALM 8:2

From the time a child is born, he or she should be surrounded by music. Indeed, these are the years of praise, when little ones learn to sing to the Lord without inhibitions. Long before children have the misfortune to learn about peer pressure or stage fright, they are free to sing and worship with pure innocence and joy. Guillaume de Machaut, the greatest sacred composer of the fourteenth century, exclaimed: "Music is a science that would have us laugh and sing and dance." If you want your child to be a long-term worshiper, then you need to bring the joy of music into these precious early years.

Perhaps you should not even wait until birth. Studies indicate that babies in the womb react positively to musical stimuli. Renowned concert pianist Glenn Gould claimed that his mother played the piano daily while she was pregnant to expose her baby to beautiful music at the earliest age possible. As you pray for these unborn babes, also surround them with the music of praise and worship.

All parents should sing to their infants—and not just nursery rhymes but the songs of the Lord. And add motion. While holding babies, you should dance while you sing, thus giving them a sense of pulsation and rhythm. Encourage clapping along with singing. Play little games with infants that contrast loud versus soft or fast versus slow. If possible, allow them to experiment (with supervision!) with any musical instruments in your house—not recommended with Stradivarius violins. By the way, studies have shown that babies respond well to background music, particularly classical music of the Baroque and Classic eras.

Children who become familiar with music at an early age will later be comfortable singing praise. A child should learn new praise songs every year. This is a great way of teaching Bible verses and stories. Adding motions will enhance the song and make it easier to memorize. Children have a far greater capacity for learning and memorizing music than is generally attempted. Each song that they sing is a double blessing: Not only are they immediately praising God but they are also setting the groundwork for a lifetime of worship.

These are indeed the years of praise, but there are other worship tools not to be forgotten. Reading Bible stories to your children is invaluable. When Paul wrote to Timothy, his commendation was that "from infancy you have known the holy scriptures" (2 Timothy 3:15). By the time children are six they can learn dozens of Bible stories, which will stay with them for life. Make certain that they understand the stories. Also be sure to teach them that that *this really happened,* to differentiate Scripture from the many fictional stories of childhood. Explain the stories at the children's levels and make them relevant for today. The stories about Jesus are particularly recommended, as they will initiate a relationship between the children and the Lord.

Finally, help your children begin to memorize Bible verses. Children of three or four can easily learn a dozen short phrases like "Jesus is Lord," "Christ is Risen" and "Glory to God." As they grow, they can learn longer verses. Use a modern translation and make certain that the meaning of each verse is clear. Reward progress generously and watch your child's spiritual progress as you sow the precious Word of God into their lives.

Ages 7 to 11: Communicating with God

"Ask and it will be given to you; seek and you will find; knock and the door will be opened to you."

MATTHEW 7:7

During this next phase of childhood, the focus in our curriculum shifts to prayer. Doubtless your child will already be familiar with praying in some form, such as the toddler's poem

> I see the moon
> And the moon sees me;
> God bless the moon
> And God bless me.

Furthermore, the child will have many times watched you and others praying during family prayer times. But now is the time when your child's prayers become his or her own, increase in fervency and become more specific and directed.

When they are little, children do not really understand whom they are praying to. During this period help them realize that prayer is truly communicating with the God who created the entire universe, and that *He is always listening.* They should realize that they are talking to the very Jesus of whom they have heard so much. A good subject to discuss is the need to pray "in Jesus' name," as the Lord commanded.

Children now can learn about the many types of prayer. Encourage them to thank God for His many blessings (thanksgiving) and pray for the Lord to help others (intercession).

When specifically asking for something (petitionary prayer), they learn to consider their own motives. James explains that when we do not receive what we pray for, it is because "you ask with wrong motives, that you may spend what you get on your pleasures" (James 4:3). We can begin to teach our children to understand what it means to pray according to God's will.

The object is that the children learn to pray *by themselves,* anywhere and in any situation. Paul taught that we should "pray continually" (1 Thessalonians 5:17) and we must model this as a reality, not an exaggeration. Too many Christians only cry out to God when trouble develops. Instead, we should train our children to pray all the time—not simply to ask for things but also in order to consistently deepen our relationship with the Lord. It is essential that your children learn prayer as a natural part of living. Remember the words of Martin Luther: "To be a Christian without prayer is no more possible than to be alive without breathing."

Although God sometimes says no to our requests, children should be inspired to believe in the power of prayer, that *prayer changes things.* Once our family had a financial need, and we prayed for God's assistance with Chris and John (ages eight and five at that time). That evening our doorbell rang, but when I opened the front door no one was there. The amount of money that we needed was in an envelope taped to the door. This blessing greatly increased our children's faith, and we were amused to hear them later discussing whether or not it was an angel who delivered the cash to us. Chris, who disagreed with this analysis, objected: "Where would an angel get that kind of money!"

Because children this age have such free imaginations, begin to direct them to "set [their] minds on things above, not on earthly things" (Colossians 3:2). Children in this period can truly begin to *imagine heaven* and this should be encouraged as it will help them never fear death. Do not give them dull images of harp playing.

166

We used to tell our children stories of all the fun we would have flying through the universe, right through the middle of stars! Compared to such heavenly adventures, anything this earth has to offer pales in comparison.

As the focus gradually changes with this new period of childhood, please do not throw out everything from the previous period. Keep the children who have entered this prayer phase of the curriculum singing and memorizing Scripture as often as possible!

Furthermore, you should now encourage your children to *read the Bible by themselves.* They should own their own Bibles and read a short portion every day. Help them to select appropriate readings, starting with the gospels and Old Testament books with a good deal of story content. Check your bookstore for age-appropriate editions, with illustrations and discussion material. Reading the Bible should be exciting and relevant to their young lives. President John Quincy Adams once wrote: "So great is my veneration for the Bible that *the earlier my children begin to read it,* the more confident will be my hope that they will prove useful citizens to their country and respectable members of society" (emphasis mine). As soon as your children begin reading, they can begin reading God's Word.

Ages 12 to 15: Digging into the Word

"Do not let this Book of the Law depart from your mouth; meditate on it day and night, so that you may be careful to do everything written in it. Then you will be prosperous and successful."

JOSHUA 1:8

The junior high years. Many parents dread them. Some even fear them. Yes, it is a time of emotional upheaval. Yes, it is a time when many kids rebel against all authority. But this can also be a beautiful time between parents and children, with much spiritual growth (on both parts).

Of course, if you treat your teenagers like ten year olds you are asking for trouble. In the same way, if you make them worship in the same way as a ten year old, you are asking for trouble. In particular, most of them do not want to sing, at least in public (especially boys). Does this make them horrible people? Does this mean that you have lost them for life? No. We have already seen that worship is much more than singing. There are many ways to worship the Lord, and other tools need to be emphasized when your children are in this age group.

The best focus is certainly the Bible itself, but again, it must be approached in the correct way. If you simply tell junior high children to "go read the Bible," you will probably see their eyes rolling. They may feel as if you are treating them like a little kid, always a mistake. As an adult who reads the Bible yourself, you may think this is strange (and you are right!). Nevertheless, many junior highers consider themselves much too cool to "go read the Bible."

This age group longs to feel "grown up," to be able to do things that older kids do. So how should we use this fact to encourage their Bible reading? Simple. You suggest Bible reading on a more difficult, adult-like scale.

I used to have a classroom of seventh- and eighth-grade boys who made it abundantly clear that they did *not* want to read the Bible. So I announced that we were doing a topical Bible study. They could hardly object since none of them knew what this meant, so they waited for me to continue. I gave them each a sheet with the word SPECK at the top, and on the left side downward, the letters S, P, E, C and K were written.

"S stands for 'sin,'" I explained. "P is for 'promise,' E for 'example,' C for 'command' and K for 'knowledge.' We're going to read Mark, chapter 2. When you see a sin to avoid, write it down next to the *S* on your paper. When you see a promise to claim, an example to follow, a command to obey or knowledge to obtain, write it down. See who can find the most of each category. You have thirty minutes. Go!"

The young men dove into the task as if they had not a moment to lose. By the time it was over, these kids who did not want to read the Bible were hotly debating whether Mark 2:17 is a promise or an example. (It is both, but I didn't tell them. It was better to let them fight it out for themselves.) They were not just reading the Bible; they were deeply engaged in every word. In the next few months we went through all four gospels using this method! By the time the class was over, these junior highers knew more about Matthew, Mark, Luke and John than some seminarians.

They were not about to "read the Bible," something that little kids might do. But these teens were strongly challenged by doing something that only an older, intelligent person could do. They were not about to sing or worship together. But they took to an "adult" Bible study like a duck to water.

Dozens of variations of the above technique can be applied. Sometimes your children should read a passage (Psalm 37 comes to mind, as well as many others) looking for two specific things: our responsibility and God's responsibility. Write every example down in two lists. Or give them three character qualities (such as diligence, generosity and humility) and find every verse in Proverbs 5 that refers to any of the three. The youth section of your Christian bookstore will give you many other ideas.

Use your imagination, but get your children digging into the Word! As they grow, it will guide their spiritual maturity. Goethe observed: "The Bible grows more beautiful, as we grow in our understanding of it." Every child is different, but in this tricky period of parenting, Bible study is probably the most effective tool to use.

If your children are especially prayerful, encourage them to intercede for others and not just themselves. Whatever you do (or whatever they do), keep the lines of communication open. Remember that *unconditional love* you promised them when they were cute and cuddly? Now that promise gets to be tested. Love them through this period and watch an amazing "young adult" appear at the other end.

Ages 16 to 19: Putting It All Together

The LORD is near to all who call on him, to all who call on him in truth.

PSALM 145:18

Before sending your teenagers off to college, you will want to spend all the time you can with them. In many ways, this is your last chance to influence them toward a lifetime of adoring God. Of course, they will still come home during college, and even as adults they will likely listen to your counsel. Nevertheless, their senior high years represent a significant period for parenting, before the critical jump toward independence.

It is during this important window of time—between the turbulent years of adolescence and the independent years of early adulthood—when worship patterns are often established for life. It is while the concrete is still drying and not completely set that we are given one last time to guide and influence. It is sad to see parents throw up their hands during the junior high rebellions and, therefore, miss the growing maturity of their teens. Sometimes this growth is rather difficult to detect! Yet it is there, and it is actually increasing. During this critical time, while maturity is emerging, we can help establish a lifetime of worship.

What part of the curriculum should they be majoring in at this time? Not one specific area, but the integration of it all.

This is when we bring together a good balance of worship tools, specifically the balance of worship, prayer and the Bible. You must (carefully) be aware of how these three items are finding space in your teen's life. The best approach is usually indirect. Rather than barge in with a question like "How's your prayer life?" you must discern this situation during normal conversation. Only after speaking about passages from the Word that have impressed you recently would it be natural to ask, "What have you been reading lately?"

When you find that there is a deficiency in one of these three areas, further delicacy is required. This is *not* the time to command: "You had better be praying more!" Sometimes a joint project can be suggested. If your teen is not in the Bible with consistency, perhaps the two of you could memorize something together, such as a psalm or particular teachings of Jesus.

The idea is to do something *together*. Most teenagers, especially after getting their driver's licenses, are rarely home as often as when they were little. Parents are busy, too! I urge parents of teens, therefore, to *make* time to spend together, preferably one-on-one time.

In the times when you are together, talk about your own worship life. Tell them (in a natural, not preachy voice) what "works for you." When I casually mention a "worship walk" that I have recently taken, I am creating a subtle suggestion that they might do the same. This is much more effective than *telling* them to do so. When I give thanks for an answered prayer, I am indirectly influencing them to pray and believe God for answers to prayer. Do not be preachy. Be an example they can follow.

Many times throughout this book, we have considered the importance of *modeling*, of living a lifestyle of worship before your children. As Paul said to his disciples, we have said, in effect, to our children, "Follow my example, as I follow the example of Christ" (1 Corinthians 11:1). This will always be relevant, even after your children have become adults. Yet as they emerge from adolescence, we need to encourage them to focus—not on us or our example—but on Christ Himself. More than ever before, they need a living, active friendship with the Lord.

SPECIAL TIMES WITH YOUR CHILDREN

You may have already heard of a great idea for you and your children: date nights. That is, dad takes daughter out on a date and mom takes son out on a date. That's right, a real date! This should include a nice dinner and should be as special an evening as possible. Not only will the children learn how to treat the opposite sex properly, but this will also give opportunities for some meaningful, uninterrupted conversation.

To develop that idea further, consider other special days for mom and dad to spend time alone with the children. I am referring here to an exceptional day that can be planned in advance and anticipated by each child. The Bible tells us, "As iron sharpens iron, so one man sharpens another" (Proverbs 27:17). In the same way, the dynamic of having one parent with one child for this length of time is phenomenal. These days can be true turning points in your parenting. Of course, parents of large families will have to be creative to arrange such extended one-on-one time, but the benefits for your children can be life-changing.

One of these special days for the young child might be the time when you explain at length what used to be called "the birds and the bees." Obviously, your explanations about the manner in which God created the two sexes will not take an entire day. The first half of this day should be spent in fun and games. Ideally, dad should take each son on such an outing, and mom each daughter, though this is not always possible. Whatever way you plan it, making this a special day will help to emphasize the significance of a godly and accurate perspective on such an important topic.

When your child is a bit older, another time for a special day could be called "preparing for adolescence." For years I have used and recommended the excellent tape series of that name by Dr. James Dobson (Focus on the Family), but a variety of materials is available. Again, one parent with one child is the best formula. Part of the day should be spent having fun and part listening to tapes and having a forthright discussion. This can be one of the most valuable opportunities to avoid many of the typical problems that develop during the teen years.

It is also advisable to have a special day together before your teenager leaves for college, particularly if this involves a move away from home. This is *not* for the purpose of a "warning harangue"—that is, "Don't do this!" and "Don't do that!" Quite the contrary. It is a time to cement relationships and communication, without which the college years can be nightmarish for all involved. For this day to have fullest effect, the parent must be vulnerable and approachable, sharing appropriately from his or her past (successes and failures) to give these budding young adults perspective about life ahead.

There are many variations of this practice, and every parent must prayerfully seek what is best for each family. The principle is simple: Save these special days for the life teachings you consider the most important of all. You do not need a special day to explain that you are buying another car. But you might if you are buying a new house, especially if the move takes your children away from their school and neighborhood friends. Use your judgment, and save these special days for the turning points of parenting.

SENDING YOUR CHILDREN OFF
TO A LIFETIME OF WORSHIP

Anyone who tries to raise children to adore God sometimes has to deal with feelings of guilt. The reason is simple: We have each failed in some capacity of parenting. We all have. If you do not know this, then you have not tried yet. When we fail at being a model parent, we pick ourselves up, ask for forgiveness and try again. Yet, as fallible parents, we are still aware of our failures.

When a teenage child makes a mistake in judgment, many a conscientious parent will wring his hands and ask himself, "Where did I go wrong? What can I do now? I've ruined him for life!" Thankfully, this is not true in most cases. Teens in particular tend to make a lot of poor choices, most of which are temporary in consequence. Still, our parental guilt lingers on.

What should we do with such guilt and worry? How can we send our children off into the world with confidence when we know that some of their future mistakes may trace themselves back to mistakes in our parenting? Perhaps the apostle Paul gives us the best model for our attitude about this.

In 2 Timothy 4:7–8, Paul, late in his life, examines his previous years of ministry:

> I have fought the good fight, I have finished the race, I have kept the faith. Now there is in store for me the crown of righteousness, which the Lord, the righteous Judge, will award to me on that day—and not only to me, but also to all who have longed for his appearing.

Almost twenty centuries later, we read these words and nod approvingly, since we recognize the greatness of Paul's ministry. Yet it might help us to ask the question: Did Paul ever make mistakes in his ministry? Yes, he surely did. Of course, as Bible-believing Christians we firmly trust that the Holy Spirit inspired every word of his New Testament writings. But Paul was not the Lord Jesus! He was an imperfect person like ourselves, trying with all his heart to follow Christ in every way, but making mistakes and trusting God to make up for them. To believe that Paul never made any mistakes in his life is rather strange theology.

He knew his own mistakes, yet as he saw his ministry coming to a close, Paul was able to say, "I have fought the good fight, I have finished the race, I have kept the faith." Perhaps we should as well. When it is time for our children to leave the nest, we need to follow Paul's example.

If you have sincerely attempted to model a life of adoration before your children, then you have done your parenting duty before the Lord. Ultimately, we must always remember that *they are God's children first*. They are loaned to us for a limited time so that they might be guided in the ways of the Lord. But children are free agents and each will stand before God on his or her own. When they make mistakes, they will not be able to blame them on you any more than you will be able to blame yours on their grandparents.

Consider your heart. The very act of buying and reading a book such as this one is evidence that you are trying to be a godly parent. Our Lord sees your heart and He "is not unjust; he will not forget your work and the love you have shown him as you have helped his people [including your children!] and continue to help them" (Hebrews 6:10).

As you watch your older child drive off to college or the new job, remember Paul's words. Have faith that the many seeds you have planted in your child for adoring the Lord will bear great fruit. And if you sometimes struggle with guilt for past parenting mistakes, re-offer your children to God and trust Him to watch over them. Believe His promise, that there is in store for you the crown of righteousness, given to all Christian parents who steadfastly attempt to raise children to adore God.

PATRICK KAVANAUGH is the author of many books, including *The Spiritual Lives of the Great Composers* (Zondervan), *Worship—A Way of Life* (Chosen), *Raising Musical Kids* (Vine), *Music of the Great Composers* (Zondervan), *Spiritual Moments with the Great Composers* (Zondervan), *The Music of Angels: A Listener's Guide to Sacred Music, from Chant to Christian Rock* (Loyola), *You Are Talented!* (Chosen) and *Devotions from the World of Music* (Cook). He also written many articles for such publications as *National Review, Focus on the Family* and *Charisma*.

Dr. Kavanaugh now serves as executive director of the Christian Performing Artists' Fellowship, representing over one thousand members from fifty different denominations. He is also artistic director of the MasterWorks Festival and director of music at Patrick Henry College. For three years he was appointed to music panels of the National Endowment for the Arts, and he has appeared on many music and talk shows, both radio and TV.

Patrick Kavanaugh's musical education includes a doctor of musical arts and a master of music (both from the University of Maryland, where he was awarded a full graduate fellowship for three years) and a bachelor of music from the CUA School of Music. He has also done extensive post-doctoral work in musicology, music theory and conducting.

He resides in Haymarket, Virginia, with his wife, Barbara, a cellist, and their four children.

To contact Dr. Kavanaugh:

The Christian Performing Artists' Fellowship
P.O. Box 800
Haymarket, VA 20168
Phone: (703) 753-0334
Fax: (703) 753-0336
CPAF@erols.com